Terrace House 2 in Ephesos
an archaeological guide

homer*kitabevi*

T.C. KÜLTÜR VE TURİZM BAKANLIĞI

BMWF^a
Bundesministerium für Wissenschaft und Forschung

ÖAI
ÖSTERREICHISCHES
ARCHÄOLOGISCHES
INSTITUT

ÖAW
Österreichische Akademie
der Wissenschaften

General Sponsors

Vehbi Koç Foundation

SÜZER VAKFI

BORUSAN MAKİNA · CAT

alpler

dere construction

ABDİ İBRAHİM

ASSAN ALÜMİNYUM

TURGUT®

Borusan Otomotiv
BMW · MINI · LAND ROVER

ALARKO

ÜMRAN BORU

Project Sponsors

SABANCI VAKFI

TEKFEN VAKFI

Fondazione
Arvedi Buschini

ENKA VAKFI/FOUNDATION

Eczacıbaşı

DOĞUŞ GRUBU

EPHESUS FOUNDATION

TERRACE HOUSE 2
IN EPHESOS
an archaeological guide

Sabine Ladstätter

In collaboration with Barbara Beck-Brandt,
Martin Steskal and Norbert Zimmermann

Translated by Nicole M. High
in collaboration with Emma Sachs

homer*kitabevi*

ISBN: 978-9944-483-52-0

Terrace House 2 in Ephesos

Sabine Ladstätter

In collaboration with Barbara Beck-Brandt, Martin Steskal and
Norbert Zimmermann

Translated by
Nicole M. High in collaboration with Emma Sachs

Book Design by
Sinan Turan

Prepared by
Homer Kitabevi

Printed by
Altan Basım Ltd.
100. Yıl Mah. Matbacılar Sitesi No: 222/A, Bağcılar/İstanbul
Certificate No.: 11968

First Published 2013

© Homer Kitabevi ve Yayıncılık Ltd. Şti.
Certificate No.: 16972

Homer Kitabevi ve Yayıncılık Ltd. Şti.
Yeni Çarşı Cad. No: 12/A
Galatasaray 34433 İstanbul

Tel: (0212) 249 59 02 - 292 42 79
Faks: (0212) 251 39 62
e-mail: homer@homerbooks.com
wwww.homerbooks.com

North wall of the theater room (SR 6) in residential unit 1 ▶

Foreword by the author

2012 marked the 50th anniversary of the discovery of Terrace House 2 in Ephesos. The Roman private houses in the center of the ancient city of Ephesos have become a true attraction since their discovery, especially with their accessibility through the construction of the modern shelter.

In my capacity as a long-standing member of the Austrian excavations in Ephesos, and since 2009 as the director of the Austrian Archaeological Institute, and also as excavation director, it is always a pleasure to introduce interested visitors to this unique monument of Roman domestic culture. This companion through Terrace House 2 developed out of many tours and lectures. It not only presents and explains the visible archaeological remains but also provides pertinent background information. Since a compact guide cannot explain every detail, I have based the text on questions asked during visits to the Terrace House.

I recommend that you open the book to "Self-Guided Tour of Terrace House 2" when you visit the site. All of the remaining chapters are richly illustrated so that you may consult this book outside the field or at a later time.

In order to answer as many questions as possible, there is a glossary at the end of this book with the most important terms. The numbering of the rooms follows the order assigned to them during the excavations.

Sabine Ladstätter
Vienna, June 2013

Introduction

Terrace House 2, in the center of the city of Ephesos, is a 4000 m² apartment block that was divided into seven residential units on three terraces. Due to its excellent preservation, Terrace House 2 is considered one of the scientifically most important and remarkable monuments of Roman domestic culture. Not only is it possible to analyze floor plan typology, chronology and stylistic development; the Terrace House is also an inexhaustible source of evidence for material culture in the Roman period.

A series of earthquakes shook Ephesos around AD 270/280, causing a sudden destruction that allows us today to gain insight into the last decorative systems and phases of use of the Roman domestic houses. Objects discovered by archaeologists in the burnt layers directly on the ancient floors have made it possible to reconstruct various facets of life.

A particularly interesting aspect of the study of Terrace House 2 is the possibility of tracking changes in its history of use over a course of 200 years – from the development of the housing complex around AD 25-50 up until its destruction around AD 270/280. Through the building history of the separate apartments, the 'Residential Units', and their modifications, we can observe the shifts of architectural and decorative styles, as well as the changing economic and social circumstances of the inhabitants.

Overall, Terrace House 2 has revealed findings that are unique in the eastern Mediterranean.

Ephesos from the Refoundation of Lysimachus to the Turkish Period

The Magnesian Gate

A new chapter in the history of Ephesos began with its refoundation in the reign of Lysimachus (360–281 BC), a general and successor of Alexander the Great.

Fig. 1: Aerial view of Ephesos

A new chapter in the history of Ephesos began with its refoundation in the reign of Lysimachus (360-281 BC), a general and successor of Alexander the Great. The gridded city was named Arsinoeia after Arsinoë, the wife of Lysimachus, and was furnished with a network of streets that run at right angles and regularized building activity (*fig. 1*). However, scarce archaeological evidence from the high Hellenistic period (3rd century BC) suggests that the concept of this very generously planned area was not always followed: in reality, only parts of the city were built up and in use. The monumental, 9 km long city wall of the Hellenistic period is still visible today; it followed the rocky slope of both the city's hills, the Bülbüldağ and the Panayırdağ. The population of the so-called new city con-

Shortly after the death of Lysimachus in 281 BC, the city reclaimed its former name Ephesos and the settlers from the neighboring cities returned to their hometowns.

sisted of the inhabitants of the settlements by the Artemision and the Panayırdağ as well as the neighboring cities Teos, Lebedus and Colophon. The resettlement was not voluntary, and the citizens struggled against the synoecism, the joining of the settlements, ordered by those in charge.

The reason for the refoundation of Ephesos/Arsinoeia is multifaceted: King Lysimachus wanted to become independent of the temple priests of Artemis and intended to set up a counterbalance to the powerful sanctuary. Additionally, the settlement by the Artemision faced the permanent danger of high tide and floods. Moreover, the dissolution of the small city-states and the development of a central city would result in a streamlined bureaucracy and a simplified defensive system.

Shortly after the death of Lysimachus in 281 BC, the city reclaimed its former name Ephesos and the settlers from the neighboring cities returned to their hometowns. The new Ephesian city remained and served as the foundation for further urban development. The following decades were marked by changing power relations, mainly between the Seleucids and

Fig. 2: The Great Theater

Ptolemies, who fought for domination of the region.

In the early 2nd century BC, intensified Roman influence and military presence becomes noticeable. Roman armies laid siege to Ephesos multiple times but were not able to capture the city. Finally King Antiochus III was defeated by the Roman general Lucius Cornelius Scipio; according to the peace agreement of Apameia (188 BC), the Seleucid king agreed to clear Asia Minor to the Taurus River. This region, including Ephesos, was incorporated into the Pergamene Empire under Eumenes II, who had supported the Romans during the preceding military conflict. Ephesos retained its legal status as a free city, controlling a large part of the surrounding countryside and serving as a regional center for administration of the Pergamene kingdom. The

In the early 2nd century BC, intensified Roman influence and military presence becomes noticeable.

expansion of the Ephesian harbor under the Pergamene kings proved to be of particularly far-reaching importance. When the last Pergamene king, Attalos III, died without heirs, in his will he bequeathed his empire and his wealth to the Roman people.

To date, only a few Ephesian monuments, such as the Great Theater (*fig. 2*), can be dated to the Hellenistic period. Similarly, the material culture of Ephesos in the Hellenistic period is difficult to describe due to a paucity of evidence. Influence from the Greek mainland, particularly Athens, as well as Egypt and Pergamon can be detected, but the cultural development does also exhibit independent characteristics. In the course of the 2nd century BC, a high-quality craftwork developed with a large export radius. At approximately the same time, extensive building activity started to bring about profound changes in the cityscape.

Immediately following the death of Attalus III (133 BC), an anti-Roman rebellion under the leadership of Aristonicus upset the region. The city of Ephesos sided with the Romans, eventually victorious, and subsequently received the status of a civitas libera et immunis following the installation of the province Asia in 129 BC. The city enjoyed tax sovereignty, organized its own jurisdiction, and was managed by self-appointed authorities.

Ephesos had fully-functioning harbors, was very well located for traffic and controlled a large city area yet to be developed as well as a fertile hinterland that guaranteed the supply of the metropolis. It is not surprising, therefore, that Roman rule ushered in a political and economic boom that can also be seen in contemporary material culture. The appeal of the city and its surroundings is reflected in the intensified settlement of Italian merchants, who participated in urban and regional organizations.

As exploitation by Roman tax collectors became an increasing burden, with heavy de-

Immediately following the death of Attalus III (133 BC), an anti-Roman rebellion under the leadership of Aristonicus upset the region.

mands and sometimes brutal actions, the local population was driven into the arms of King Mithridates VI Eupator of Pontus (ca. 134-63 BC), who seized the coastal cities in the course of his expansion. Mithridates barely encountered any resistance and instead was praised in many places as "savior". In Ephesos the anti-Roman attitude also prevailed and led to attacks that peaked in the so-called Asiatic Vespers in 88 BC: according to ancient sources, 80,000 Italians were violently killed in Asia Minor in just one night. The Romans promptly reacted to the uprisings with intensified military strength. After the victory over Mithridates, despite the fact that the Ephesians had already adopted a pro-Roman line in 86 BC, a criminal court stripped the city of its freedom for decades. Publius Servilius Isauricus (46-44 BC), celebrated as benefactor, ultimately gave Ephesos its independence and restored its original status.

The decades after the death of Gaius Julius Caesar (44 BC) saw further turmoil in the provinces which were alternately claimed and exploited by the Caesar-assassins and their opponents. Marcus Antonius and Cleopatra set up camp in Ephesos where they spent the winter of 33/32 BC; 300 senators also joined them there in attempts of establishing a counter-senate. The victory of Gaius Caesar Octavianus in the battle of Actium in 31 BC finally relieved the situation in the highly contested province of Asia and its capital city Ephesos.

In the 1st century BC, multiple honorary monuments developed along the so-called Curetes Street of which the Memmius Monument

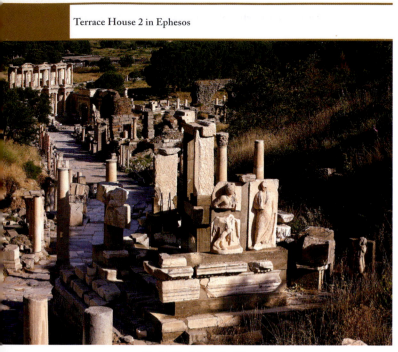

Fig. 3: The Memmius Monument

(*fig. 3*) and the Heroon of the mythical found-er Androcles still remain. The street was also lined with tabernae and richly furnished housing quarters. Although the historical development of the buildings has not yet been completely understood, the archaeological remains clearly indicate that already in the late Hellenistic pe-riod, i.e. the 2nd and 1st centuries BC, the upper Agora, the so-called State Agora, was the seat of the city administration (*fig. 4*) and the lower Agora, the so-called Tetragonos Agora, was likely the commercial center.

The accession of Gaius Caesar Octavianus (27 BC), who would become the emperor Au-gustus, initiated a period of commercial pros-perity in Ephesos. As the capital of the province Asia Minor, rich in raw materials and highly de-

In the 1st century BC, multiple honorary monuments developed along the so-called Curetes Street of which the Memmius Monument and the Heroon of the mythical founder Androcles still remain.

veloped, Ephesos quickly developed into one of the largest and most powerful metropoleis of the eastern Mediterranean. Excellent infrastructure was prerequisite for this development, including a functioning harbor (*fig. 5*) and a transport network that connected the city with its hinterland. Ephesos became extremely appealing to business people and craftsmen of varying origins and in consequence the city not only increased in population but also established itself as a commercial hub and zone of cultural contact between

Fig. 4: The upper Agora

east and west. As the residence and seat of the provincial governor, other administrators as well as the center of the provincial administration, the city required many buildings that demonstrated its wealth and power, public administrative offices and services. The Artemision was closely connected to but still spatially separated from the city and constituted the cultic and religious center. Additionally, the importance of the Artemision as a commercial locus of the region can hardly be exaggerated (*fig. 6*): the sanctuary was the proprietor of the products of large estates and natural resources from the hinterland. Furthermore, the control of coastal fishing was one of the duties of the temple priests. Due to its privileged function as a bank, the Artemision had access to extensive financial capital that could also be invested temporarily. The goddess Artemis was omnipresent in the cityscape of Roman Ephesos: the course of the old processional way wound its way through the center of the city and was surrounded on either side by dedications, honorific

Fig. 5: The Roman harbor and the harbor channel to the modern coast of Pamucak

Additionally, the importance of the Artemision as a commercial locus of the region can hardly be exaggerated.

Fig. 6: The "Beautiful Artemis"

and burial monuments. Copies of the cult figure were set up in the Prytaneion where sacrifices were performed.

In Ephesos a massive construction phase began in the Augustan period (27 BC-AD 14). The new construction was mainly concentrated in the public and political centers such as the upper Agora as well as in the private houses along the hill slopes that were completely redeveloped. Many private donors funded public buildings and thus decisively contributed to the splendid appearance of the metropolis: for example, Gaius Sextilius Pollio, his wife Ofillia Bassa and their son Ofillius Proculus financed the basilica in the so-called State Agora and also secured the water supply of the city through the construction of an aqueduct (*fig. 7*) and a nymphaeum. The commercial market, the lower Agora, did not remain untouched: the

Fig. 7: The bridge of the Pollio Aqueduct

In the reign of the emperor Tiberius (AD 14-37), Ephesos was struck by a devastating earthquake (AD 17 or 23).

so-called South Gate of the Tetragonos Agora (*fig. 8*), impressive testimony of this new wave of construction, was donated by the imperial freedmen Mithridates and Mazeus.

The official Roman imperial cults were of particular importance for the city and were established and maintained by the people in the province as expressions of loyalty towards the Roman imperial household. Following the conquest of Asia Minor, Octavian, the later emperor Augustus, fulfilled the wish of the Romans settled there to establish a cult for the deceased Caesar, Divus Iulius, and for Dea Roma. He also allowed the Greek provincial population to honor his person in connection with the city goddess of Rome. Already under Augustus, an active ruler cult was developed in the provinces and quickly spread to Italy.

In the reign of the emperor Tiberius (AD 14-37), Ephesos was struck by a devastating earthquake (AD 17 or 23). Ephesos is missing in the list of devastated cities mentioned by the Roman historian Tacitus (Annals 2. 47), but archaeologically, numerous destruction levels can be associated with this event. This catastrophe did not hinder the further rise and tremendous development of Ephesos, however; indeed, the damage was quickly repaired and the building projects resumed.

When the apostle Paul arrived in Ephesos in the course of his missionary work in AD 52, he came in contact with a large Jewish community. The archaeological sources hardly provide any information about the history of imperial Judaism but we should imagine a large and active Jewish community when Paul's missionary trips began. The unhappy end of Paul's stay culminated in the successful rebellion of silversmiths, who were worried about their profits from the sale of small Artemis devotional objects threatened by the missionary work of Paul.

In the Flavian period (AD 69-96), Ephesos again experienced a particularly prosperous pe-

Fig. 8: The Mazeus-Mithridates Gate

Under the emperor Domitian (AD 81-96), the city established an imperial cult temple for the veneration of the Flavian imperial household.

riod. In addition to individual benefactions that were privately financed, public building projects characterized the appearance of the city. These activities focused on the harbor plain and assisted in the strengthening and improvement of the infrastructure. The Harbor Baths (*fig. 9*) were constructed in the Flavian period and are one of the largest bath-gymnasium complexes in existence; together with the adjacent Halls of Verulanus, they formed a spacious ensemble by fittingly combining personal hygiene with exercise. The installation of marble pavement on the Curetes Street, which had previously only been covered with a compact gravel layer, not only transformed the appearance of the street but also introduced a change in function: while the downtown traffic route had been used for the transportation of goods up to this point, its appearance was now embellished with honorific monuments and rich sculptural furnishings.

Under the emperor Domitian (AD 81-96), the city established an imperial cult temple for the veneration of the Flavian imperial household (*fig. 10*). The monumental building, completely obliterated down to its substructures in late antiquity, dominated the western end of the upper Agora, the so-called State Agora . There the imperial cult was maintained by the council of the

Fig. 9: The Harbor Baths

province of Asia, and the temple was overseen by a high priest who was one of the highest municipal office-holders. At first the establishment of the imperial cult was initiated by the provincial population, but it quickly developed into a political tool of control over the subjects who had to demonstrate their loyalty to the imperial household through the introduction and veneration of the cult. The imperial cult was thus less of a sign of religious piety and instead a propaganda tool of imperial politics. After the damnatio memoriae of the emperor Domitian in AD 96, his name was erased everywhere, his cult statue removed, and his veneration was transferred to the entire Flavian imperial household.

The showy splendor and commercial prosperity of Ephesos reached its climax in the 2nd century AD. At this time, the cities of Asia Minor were in competition for good reputation, prestige and importance. They attempted to surpass one another not only through the construction of representative architecture, but also through the organ-

Fig. 10: The Temple of Domitian

ization of competitions and celebrations and not least through infrastructural development and the higher quality of life associated with it. Ephesos was quite successful in this battle for prestige and renown the scholar Pliny the Elder referred to the city as the "luminary of Asia" (naturalis historia 5, 120), and the rhetorician Aelius Aristides praised it with the words: "It is extensive for whomever journeys into the interior; it is even extensive on the seacoast; it is everywhere capable of satisfying every way of life". (orationes 23, 24).

The prestigious development of the city was made possible largely through the obligation of

the wealthy urban aristocrats to the community. These responsibilities –assuming expensive administrative positions, for example, or constructing generally beneficial buildings– were voluntary, and helped promote the status and reputation of an individual patron-family. In general, these families were originally of Greek origin and character but had already received Roman citizenship generations earlier and had pursued careers in the Roman army and administration. Tiberius Claudius Aristion belonged to this group as well as the widespread families of the Vedii and Varii, which were patrons over many generations. The many fountains (*fig.*

Terrace House 2 in Ephesos

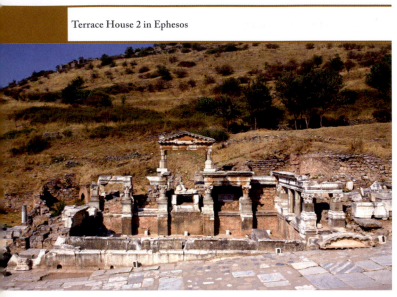

Fig. 11: The Nymphaeum of Trajan

11), baths, aqueducts, club houses, municipal buildings, and many other such buildings that shape the urbanscape of Ephesos trace back to these individuals. The most prominent example of such patronage is likely the Library of Celsus, constructed in the early 2nd century AD, that functioned as the burial monument of the patron Tiberius Julius Celsus Polemaeanus. Another important task of these urban dignitaries was the organization of games and celebrations. The gladiatorial fights were particularly popular and primarily took place in the Great Theater as well as at the stadium of Ephesos.

Under the emperor Hadrian (AD 117-138), Ephesos received permission to construct another imperial cult temple, possibly on the occasion of the imperial visit to the city in AD 129. The large flood plain near the harbor was selected for the construction of a new temple, the so-called Olympieion, for the emperor Hadrian and dedi-

Under the emperor Hadrian (AD 117-138), Ephesos received permission to construct another imperial cult temple, possibly on the occasion of the imperial visit to the city in AD 129.

Fig. 12: The adoption scene from the "Parthian Monument"

cated to Zeus Olympios. The building plot offered enough space for a monumental sanctuary (*fig. 12*). The emperor Antoninus Pius (AD 138-161) had a particularly close relationship to the province Asia as he had lived in Ephesos as the governor of the province of Asia in AD 134/135. His imperial public works included –among other things– the dredging of the silted-up harbor and its maintenance. This measure secured the lifeline of Ephesos and ensured the unimpeded transfer of goods and passage of people. The Ephesians thanked the emperor with annual celebrations and money allocations on his birthday. The Parthian War, during the co-reign of Marcus Aurelius and Lucius Verus (AD 161-169), had disastrous consequences on Ephesos: the Roman legionaries introduced the plague into

Large private dedications of this period –the early 3ʳᵈ century AD– were made by Titus Flavius Damianus and his wife Vedia Phaedrina.

Asia Minor on their return in AD 166. Over the course of 13 months, soldiers were shipped to Italy through the harbor of Ephesos; their supply was only possible through a rich grain donation by Titus Flavius Damianus.

A marked reduction in new public and private buildings can be noted in the second half of the 2ⁿᵈ century AD; frequently buildings were remodeled, adapted and renovated. On account of military needs, a large-scale street building program was implemented under the emperor Septimius Severus (AD 193-211), but the cities themselves only indirectly profited from this measure. In Ephesos the emperor was still venerated as the new Helios, the lord of the earth and seas as well as the founder of the first and largest metropolis of Asia; additionally, the construction of the third imperial cult temple for Caracalla and Geta (AD 211/212) was begun. The emperor Caracalla repealed this distinction noting that he had great respect for the Ephesian gods and ordered for his neocorate to be dedicated to Artemis instead.

Large private dedications of this period – the early 3ʳᵈ century AD– were made by Titus Flavius Damianus and his wife Vedia Phaedrina. They not only constructed the stoa of Damianus, a covered portico stretching from the Magnesian Gate to the Artemision, but they also financed a banquet hall in the Artemision as well as renovations in the gymnasia and baths. Marcus Fulvius Publicianus Nikephoros, who built the Southern Harbor Gate in his function as the asiarch and prytanis, was the last large benefactor of the imperial period.

The decline in private donations is connected to the worsening economic situation on the one hand, and on the other, a change in mentality. The individual's awareness of the community had changed, and so the pursuit of political offices and importance of outward representation had lost its attraction. This was accompanied by a lessened moral and political pressure to donate private fortunes to the public and invest in the collective. Already in the 2nd century, healing and mystery gods with distinct political characteristics took the place of the traditional, established gods, an important aspect for the history of religion. The Egyptian cults of Isis, Osiris, and Serapis were particularly popular, promising eternal life and resurrection after death.

The archaeological record of Ephesos indicates numerous earthquakes after the second quarter of the 3rd century AD that ultimately led to a break in the settlement history. Triggered by a series of earthquakes that possibly began around AD 230, the devastation of the city grew while living standards sunk. In the third quarter of the 3rd century, the earthquakes reached such a catastrophic degree that we must assume quite extensive destruction of the city. The evidence for the earthquakes extends across the entire city: reconstruction measures are visible in the Terrace Houses, in the Serapeion as well as the Prytaneion and can be linked to these natural disasters. It is a real destruction layer that encompasses the entire city and indicates a general change of the cityscape.

Furthermore in this period, the entire region was struck by raids of Gothic groups, who primarily destroyed the fertile and agriculturally important hinterland of Ephesos; thus the agricultural foundation for the supply of the city was lost. The climax of this destruction was reached with the destruction and pillaging of the Artemis temple, resulting in the faltering of belief in the great goddess and her impregnability.

The calamitous combination of earthquakes and raids ushered in long-term consequences for both the commerce of the region and the image of the city of Ephesos: due to the collapse of the infrastructure, the supply of the city was no longer ensured and a distinct decrease in population is discernible. For decades the ruins and rubble were inhabited while the building remains were only cursorily repaired. Frequently, rooms or entire sections of buildings were walled off and completely filled with rubble while the remaining areas were used in a makeshift man-

According to literary sources from the late 4th century, the Artemis temple was repaired but not fully renovated.

ner. According to literary sources from the late 4th century, the Artemis temple was repaired but not fully renovated.

There is a gap in the archaeological record in the late 3rd as well as the first half of the 4th century AD. However, by the mid-4th century, the province Asia with its capital Ephesos regained its prominence for its abundance of wine, oil, and grain. Evidence of the regained commercial prosperity are the estates in the direct vicinity of Ephesos owned by individuals from the imperial household. The production of inscriptions and sculpture resumed and various buildings were renovated. However, these renovations primarily concentrated on the public buildings in the old city center, the upper Agora, i.e. the so-called State Agora, as well as the Curetes Street (*fig. 13*).

Fig. 13: Curetes Street

A clear recovery can be detected at the end of 4th and the beginning of the 5th century but this no longer affected the upper Agora where the buildings were abandoned or functionally altered. The public space shifted to the Curetes Street which was lined with honorary inscriptions and additionally emphasized and clearly demarcated by adjoining halls and the Hercules Gate to the east. Acclamations, honorary statues and inscribed laws were prominently positioned in front of imperial monuments or were integrated into the monuments. Tabernae, located behind the halls, were used as taverns, shops and workshops. The actual administration and living districts were located in the lower city of Ephesos, particularly around the harbor. Massive building activity took place in this densely built area in Late Antiquity.

Fig. 14: The Church of Mary

Sophisticated new buildings were also produced such as the so-called Byzantine Palace.

Fig. 15: Late Antique houses in the harbor area

The building program probably included representative administrative buildings as well as –now Christian– sanctuaries, boulevards, infrastructural amenities, and commercial buildings. All available resources were at their disposal and thus the old and partially standing building remains were used and adapted for other purposes. The most prominent example is likely the Church of Mary (*fig. 14*), which was set into the elongated south hall of the Olympieion. Formerly spacious squares such as the palaestra of the Harbor Bath offered enough space to accommodate richly furnished private houses. These are, in keeping with the traditions of the Imperial period, peristyle houses with elaborate furnishings such as polychrome mosaic floors, opus sectile floors and wall paintings (*fig. 15*).

Sophisticated new buildings were also produced such as the so-called Byzantine Palace (*fig. 16*); the construction made it necessary to remove some remains of Roman houses and level the area. According to the building typology of the complex, the palace can possibly be identified as the seat of a provincial governor,

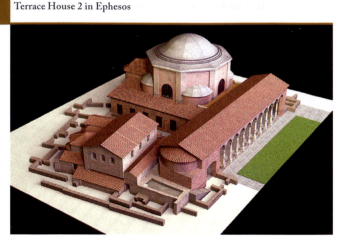

Fig. 16: The so-called Byzantine Palace

The former administrative center of the city, the upper Agora, was adapted for living use as late as the 6ᵗʰ century.

a strategos, or of a cleric, possibly even of the bishop of Ephesos.

In Late Antiquity numerous public buildings not only retained their original function but also were newly furnished. This is most clearly documented in the Late Antique use, destruction, and deterioration history of the Vedius Gymnasium (*fig. 17*), to the north of the Roman city.

Despite these renovations, ruined buildings defined the appearance of the city over a long period of time. According to the archaeological record, entire city quarters must have been covered by debris for over a century before the remains were finally removed or renovated. The former administrative center of the city, the upper Agora, was adapted for living use as late as the 6th century.

The ruins also offered rich material that could be removed and reused in other places. Architectural parts and sculptures were collected and set up in new arrangements. The boulevards profited the most from this new handling of old materials; their Late Antique appearance was marked by the decorative re-use of works of art from the Imperial period.

The harbor of Ephesos remained the lifeline of the city. Due to continual silting up and pollution from the city, the harbor basin had to be consistently maintained and cleaned so that its functionality could be upheld and so shipping could go unrestricted. These problems had been known since the late Hellenistic period, and the accumulation of mud could only be removed with great effort and the use of mechanical equipment. Already in the 1st century AD a short channel connected the artificial har-

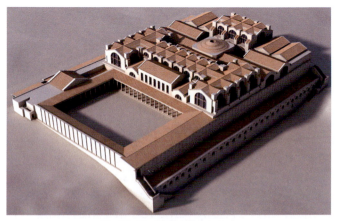

Fig. 17: The Vedius Gymnasium

The responsibility of the agriculturally used hinterland was primarily to supply the city of Ephesos with wheat, oil, and wine, but select items were exported during Late Antiquity.

bor basin with the open sea; but in the following centuries this channel became longer and narrower due to sedimentary deposition. A cemetery developed on either side of the channel and the inventory of the burials suggests that it came into use in the 3rd century (*fig. 18*). The location of the necropolis is impressive as it imitates the phenomenon of tombs lining a road –in this case a waterway– and must have been an imposing image for visitors entering the city.

In AD 431, Ephesos was designated as the venue of the 3rd ecumenical council for two crucial reasons: the city could be reached from land as well as the sea, and the city had the commercial strength to accommodate and supply all the participants. This is important evidence of the intense agricultural production of the Ephesian chora, so decisive for the prosperity of the region. The responsibility of the agriculturally used hinterland was primarily to supply the city of Ephesos with wheat, oil, and wine, but select items were exported during Late Antiquity. Ownership does not appear to have changed drastically – apart from the expropriation of the temple estates of the Artemision, which were then transferred to the public or the church.

The city territory of Ephesos was again reduced in size as early as the 7th century AD (*fig.

Fig. 18: The Harbor Necropolis

19). The so-called Byzantine City Wall was possibly also constructed in this period; it encircled the core of the settlement from the Great Theater in the south and the Vedius Gymnasium in the North to the Harbor Basin. The city gate was now situated on the marble road and was directly connected with the stage building of the theater. The Curetes Street lost its function as public center and shopping street as late as the second quarter of the 7th century. The tabernae were abandoned, and the halls along the sides of the street were closed off with dry stone walls of spolia, probably to hold back the rubble from the slope. In the area of the Terrace House 2, a workshop quarter developed, consisting of potter's workshops, smithies, a workshop for the cutting of stone and a line of mills.

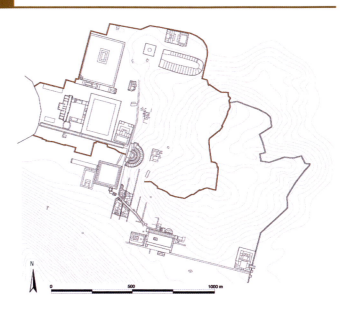

Fig. 19: Plan of the Late Antique city of Ephesos

In the course of Late Antiquity, numerous chapels and churches were built in Ephesos. The Church of Mary, used as the venue for the council, as well as the Basilica of St. John (*fig. 20*), the Cemetery of the Seven Sleepers (*fig. 21*), and the so-called Grave of St. Luke developed into centers of pilgrimage that attracted Christians, turning the city into a locus of early Christian pilgrimage. This resulted in an economic upswing of the region and was a motivator for the intensified maintenance of a functioning traffic system and ensured accessibility from the sea. In the city and the extra-urban sanctuaries, facilities were established that were geared towards providing accommodation and lodging to pilgrims. Throughout Late Antiquity, Ephesos retained its function as a supra-

In the course of Late Antiquity, numerous chapels and churches were built in Ephesos.

regional commercial center because the harbor and its channel remained in good working order over a long period of time. The city continued to be supplied with goods from many different countries and the households of the wealthy population had a high standard of living.

The city remained continually inhabited until the 14th century, as suggested by evidence from the graveyards surrounding the churches. At the same time, additional settlements developed on the Ayasoluk hill and in the former temenos of the Artemision in the 11th century and

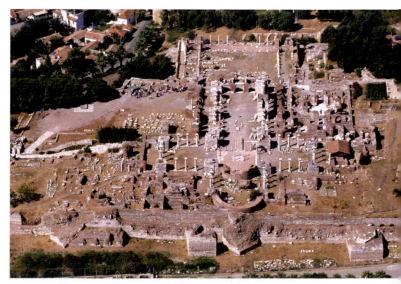

Fig. 20: The Basilica of St. John

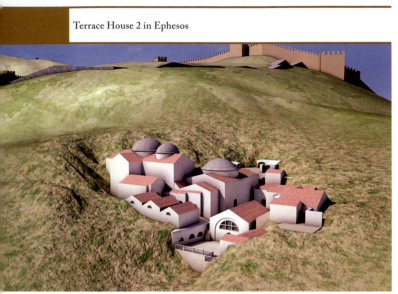

Terrace House 2 in Ephesos

Fig. 21: The Seven Sleepers Cemetery

Ayasoluk had another boom under the family of the Aydınoğulları and particularly under the learned Emir İsa Bey (1348-1390).

continue to exist today as the old town center of modern Selçuk (*fig. 22*). The Byzantine settlers were able to defend themselves against the Seljuk attacks with the military support of the new commercial powers of the Mediterranean: the Genoese and the Venetians. It is uncertain how long the Ephesian harbor remained usable. In any case, additional ports and trading posts developed along the coast near the modern settlement of Pamucak, and also to the south.

The Christian-Byzantine rule in Ephesos ended in 1304 when the entire region was captured by the Seljuks and first belonged to the emirate of Aydın. Ayasoluk had another boom under the family of the Aydınoğulları and particularly under the learned Emir İsa Bey (1348-1390).

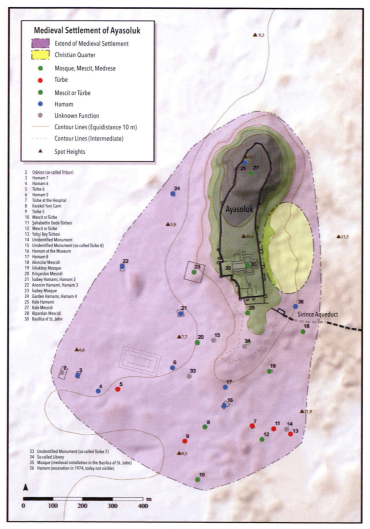

Fig. 22: Plan of the Turkish city Ayasoluk

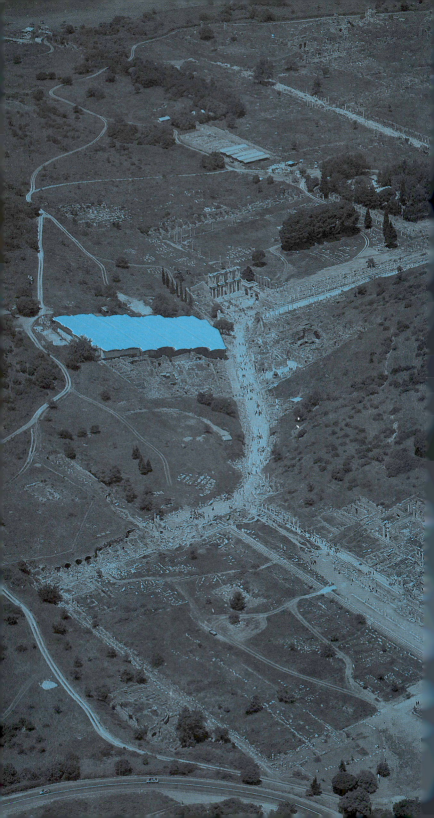

Topography and the Incorporation of Terrace House 2 into the Urban Fabric

Fig. 23: Aerial view of the Terrace Houses

Terrace House 2 refers to an apartment complex in the center of the Roman city of Ephesos. The insula measures 4,000 m² and was built into the steep north slope of the Bülbüldağ, the southern hill of Ephesos (fig. 23).

To the west and east, the insula is surrounded by buildings comparable in construction and furnishing; of these only Terrace House 1 to the east has been excavated and studied. Additional Roman private houses were excavated on the opposite slope on the Panayırdağ, south of the Great Theater, and below the so-called Byzantine Palace. Geophysical prospection in various city quarters has revealed insula-buildings spread across the entire city.

Terrace House 2 is delimited to the south by the so-called Terrace House Street with a west-east axis and to the north by the Curetes Street. The irregular course of the former processional way –the street now referred to as the Curetes Street– did not adhere to the regular plan of the gridded city, and this explains the trapezoidal ground plan of the insula. On the eastern and western sides, the structure is bound by two stepped alleys with an elevation of 27 m and from which the Residential Units could be accessed.

Originally 6 Residential Units were constructed on three terraces of comparable size, measuring between 400 and 600 m². At their

northern end, taber-
nae, used as shops
or taverns, faced the
street and opened
up onto the Curetes
Street. The tabernae
were separated from
the street by a row
of late Hellenistic
and Imperial honor-
ific monuments that

Fig. 24: The Octagon, virtual reconstruction

lined the processional way. In addition to the
Androcles Heroon, the Octagon was prominent in the cityscape (*fig. 24*). The Octagon
is a tomb of the Augustan period where Arsinoë IV, the sister of Cleopatra the Great, was
buried. The exclusivity of the district was increased by the construction of the temple of
Hadrian and the Library of Celsus as well as
the paving of the Curetes Street with marble
slabs during the Roman Imperial period.

The location of the Terrace House 2 in the
center of the Roman city of Ephesos suggests that its residents belonged to an urban
elite with enough funds to purchase property in this prominent district. The separate
Residential Units of the Terrace House were
the urban residences of prominent wealthy
Ephesian citizens whose houses did not only
have private functions but were also used for
business, the reception of clients and guests,
as well as the general representation of the
owners.

The Investigation of
Terrace House 2

Fig. 25: Terrace House 2 at the beginning of excavation

*T*he first rooms of the Terrace House 2 were discovered in 1962 (fig. 25) when one of the most famous wall paintings, the Socrates fresco, came to light.

The fresco was removed from the wall according to the standards of the time and has been on view ever since in the Efes Müzesi in Selçuk (*fig. 47*). The extensive and continuous excavation of the insula began in 1967 under the direction of Hermann Vetters, who assumed the responsibility of director of the excavations in Ephesos two years later. Due to his leadership, the Terrace House 2 became the focus of the archaeological excavations in Ephesos and remained so up until his retirement as excavation director in 1985.

The archaeologists had to overcome many challenges in the excavation of the living quarters. The high layers of Roman debris covering the Roman ruins had to be removed as well as the younger settlement phases and burials from the Byzantine and Turkish periods had to be cleared away in order to reach the Roman layers. In the first years of excavation, about 100 workmen, with the aid of heavy machinery (*fig. 26*), removed sometimes up to 5,000 m³ of dirt at a time. Beginning in the south, Residential Units 1 and 2 were excavated first, revealing the excellent state of preservation of the buildings. Almost all of the rooms were decorated either with wall painting or with marble panel revetment, the floors covered with mosaics. Many furnishings were also preserved under the destruction layers; these were recovered and moved to the museum in Selçuk. The Residential Units were quickly excavated, one after another, from south to north, and every year both the public and the archaeological community were surprised by the sensational finds. When Hermann Vetters retired, giving up his position as director of the excavations at the end of the excavation season in 1985, Terrace House 2 was completely excavated but not yet fully analyzed.

Thanks to the commitment of Friedrich Krinzinger, the excavation director of Ephesos from 1998-2007, the investigation of Terrace House 2 was intensified and incorporated into the research program of the Institute for the Study of Ancient Culture of the Austrian Academy of Sciences in Vienna. In the course of the research project, further excavations took place to clarify older building phases; the architecture and the rich find material were also analyzed. The results have been presented in multiple comprehensive volumes in the series "Forschungen in Ephesos".

Fig. 26: Terrace House 2 during excavation

The Preservation of the Remains:
"A Roof for Ephesos"

Fig. 27: The minimal roofing of Terrace House 2 during excavation

◀ The steel construction of the protective roof

Fig. 28: The protective shelter around Residential Units 1 and 2

*A*lthough the scientific and cultural relevance of Terrace House 2 is undisputed, its conservation and restoration has been extremely challenging.

The wall paintings recovered during the initial discovery of Terrace House 2 were removed and brought to the local museum in Selçuk. In the course of the intense excavation work in the 1970s and 80s, the objects were simply left in place due to the wealth of surface decoration. Despite continual preservation measures taken during excavation, it was impossible to prevent deterioration from various climatic conditions: particularly the rainy winters and the intense sun in the summer. Already in the first years of the excavation the necessity of a sun shelter was recognized, and in addition to conservation efforts, the idea of a museum installation existed from the start. The stated goal was to create a museum in the ruins, to present the excavated objects in their original context and to explain and present the archaeological record on-site.

It took 38 years, and many discussions and drafts until the now existing protective structure was built under the slogan "A Roof for Ephesos".

At first the decision was made to cover individual rooms and groups of rooms (*fig. 27*), but the appearance of these roofs was soon criticized. In the late 1970s, a project was completed that recreated the 3rd dimension based on the ground plan so that the ancient sense of space as well as the original lighting could be recreated for visitors (*fig. 28*). The roof was covered with tiles so that the aesthetic of the ruins of Ephesos would not be destroyed. While the excavations of the Residential Units 6 and 7 continued on the northern terrace, the protective building was begun in the south. Terrace House 2 was made partially publicly accessible for the first time for its opening ceremony in 1985. However, concerns over the choice of reinforced concrete as the building material interrupted the project in 1986 and then completely halted it. The reasons for this stop were the unfavorable climate for the ancient materials as well as concerns about the overall aesthetic impact, particularly on the roofscape.

It took 38 years, and many discussions and drafts until the now existing protective structure was built under the slogan "A Roof for Ephesos". With the help of numerous large

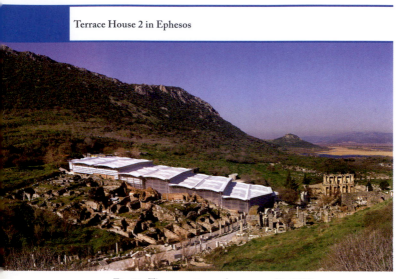

Fig. 29: The protective roof, constructed in 2000

donors, including the exceptional initiative of the Gesellschaft der Freunde von Ephesos, the monument could again be presented to the public (*fig. 29*). A so-called booklet of specifications defined the requirements for the current protective building: it must differ from the building elements of Terrace House 2 in construction, color and choice of material and should visually recede, emphasizing the ruins. Additional imperative functions included its effective protection against the weather and its reversibility and deconstruction. With special consideration of the mistakes of the past, the climatic conditions were specifically considered. The roofing material was supposed to be a breathable, UV-repellent, stable "skin" stretched across the building, allowing for natural ventilation. The result is a stainless steel construction (*fig. 30*) that is only minimally invasive to the ancient material. The gill-shaped façade of sheets of Lexan, a type

The Preservation of the Remains: "A Roof for Ephesos"

Additional imperative functions included its effective protection against the weather and its reversibility and deconstruction. With special consideration of the mistakes of the past, the climatic conditions were specifically considered.

Fig. 30: The steel construction of the protective roof

of polycarbonate, facilitate the constant ventilation and are thus crucial for the balanced climate inside (*fig. 31*). The roof is covered by a textile, a glass-fiber reinforced membrane with a Teflon coating that promised to be self-cleaning, extremely strong, and have a long lifecycle.

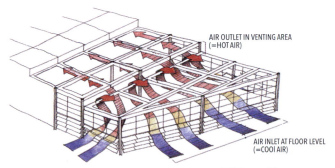

AIR OUTLET IN VENTING AREA
(=HOT AIR)

AIR INLET AT FLOOR LEVEL
(=COOl AIR)

Fig. 31: Model of air flow patterns in the roofed Terrace House 2

The unique monument has been open to the public since 2006 and in 2012 over 150,000 tourists –less than 5% of all visitors to Ephesos– toured Terrace House 2.

The Turkish authorities built footbridges and steps into the inside of the Terrace House in order to guide visitors and provide an impressive view into Roman private architecture (*fig. 32*). The interior appearance of the new construction is noteworthy as it visually recedes and emphasizes the ancient remains. The reconstruction of ancient remains was consciously avoided: the lighting and path does not reflect the Roman reality. With the

Fig. 32: Visitor path inside Terrace House 2

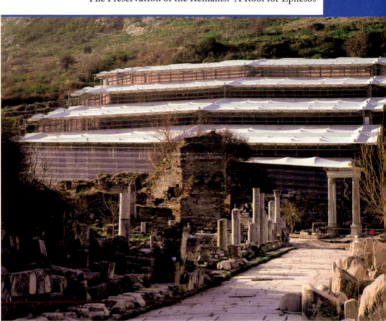

Fig. 33: The protective shelter viewed from the north

help of the visitor guidance system, illusionary impressions and overviews are created that allow for completely new and unexpected perceptions of the remains on view. The unique monument has been open to the public since 2006 and in 2012 over 150,000 tourists –less than 5% of all visitors to Ephesos– toured Terrace House 2 (*fig. 33*). A museum was created in the ruins of Ephesos that not only protects but also makes the monument accessible. Furthermore, the roofing makes it possible to have a year-round conservation season irrespective of weather. The monument is also a workshop and offers the visitor the possibility of immediate contact with science and research.

Conservation and Restoration Work in Terrace House 2

Fig. 34: The 'Erotes Room' (18) before conservation

*T*he shelter over Terrace House 2 and the well-designed visitor path permit the realization of a sustainable conservation concept alongside the scientifically-founded presentation of the ruins.

Fig. 35: The 'Erotes Room' (18) after conservation

Furthermore, the proximity of conservators and visitors gives the interested visitors insight into the work processes and possibly promotes understanding for the conservation measures that often appear tedious and seem to proceed slowly.

The basis for the work is a maintenance concept in the course of which the current state of the monument is continually monitored so that possible changes including deterioration can immediately be remedied. A mapping of the current state of the wall

This revealed that the paintings are not only exposed to temperature and humidity fluctuations but also exhibit dust and pollution deposits and thus need to be cleaned annually.

Fig. 36: Bird motif before conservation

Fig. 37: Bird motif after conservation

paintings –irrespective of their artistic or cultural value– was begun, including a loss assessment and a set of measures so that preventative conservation can take place. Based on this analysis, the consolidation and partial restoration in six rooms (16a, 17, 18, 27, 36 and 36a) took place until 2013 (*fig. 34. 35*). This revealed that the paintings are not only exposed to temperature and humidity fluctuations but also exhibit dust and pollution deposits and thus need to be cleaned annually. In all rooms, cracks and gaps can be found that –similar to the deformations and the detachment of plaster layers– are the result of the numerous earthquakes. The colors appear altered through their preservation in the soil and the organic components of veg-

The marble panels fell off of the walls in the course of the earthquake (AD 270/280) and were discovered by the archaeologists in the rubble and on the floor of the room.

etable origin (*fig. 36. 37*). Earlier practices such as the addition of substances containing salt and cement caused a recrystallization film that appears as grey-white streaking throughout the wall paintings. Microorganisms are also prevalent and equally deteriorate the ancient substance.

The current work on the wall paintings consists first of strengthening the parts in danger of collapsing, then the loose dirt is

Fig. 38: The stabilization of the surface of the painting

Conservation and Restoration Work in Terrace House 2

Fig. 39: The conservation project in the Marble Hall (31)

removed, and finally, gaps are filled with mortar (*fig. 38*). Following the cleaning, all gaps and edges are puttied with mortar of fine lime and additives. Finally, they are re-touched with water colors.

A second ongoing conservation project since 2007 is the reconstruction and mounting of marble wall revetments in the Marble Hall (room 31) of Residential Unit 6. The marble panels fell off of the walls in the course of the earthquake (AD 270/280) and were discovered by the archaeologists in the rubble and on the floor of the room. In a first work process all of the fragments were viewed, cleaned and categorized. It was necessary to remove the stubborn dirt and

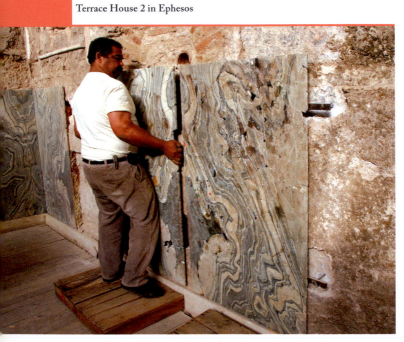

Fig. 40: Mounting the glued marble panels on the wall

The work in the main and upper zone was not yet complete in 2012, but 14 pavonazetto panels as well as the pilasters and capitals have already been assembled and partially glued together.

plaster adhesions with scalpel and spatula. This treatment was applied to 120,000 fragments in total (*fig. 39*): 10,000 from the lowest zone (cipollino verde), 70,000 from the middle zone (pavonazetto), and 40,000 from the upper opus sectile zone.

The cipollino-verde panels were glued with an epoxy resin and the gaps were filled with plaster. 2 cm thick Aerolam sheets were inserted into larger gaps with epoxy resin. A moveable rail system was developed for the mounting on the walls, thus making it possible to move the slabs from inside to outside over adjustable steel dowels (*fig. 40*). This system guarantees reversibility, but also flexibility during the mounting process, and protects the panels from future earthquake damage through the space to the wall.

The work in the main and upper zone was not yet complete in 2013 (*fig. 41*), but 14 pavonazetto panels as well as the pilasters and capitals have already been assembled and partially glued together. The mounting on the wall is close to the original through the

Fig. 41: The Pavonazetto panels after reassembly

The inscriptions discovered on the backs of the slabs were not only indicative of the exact chronological classification of the marble decoration, but they are also an important source for the marble trade in the Roman Imperial period, for the building process in the Marble Hall itself and not least for questions of ownership in Terrace House 2.

comparison of ancient dowel traces that still exist on the slabs as well as on the wall.

The reconstruction of the opus sectile panels was particularly challenging (*fig. 42*) because they were broken into very small fragments. According to the reconstruction state in 2012, we assume that there were at least 12 panels with central emblemata made of Porfido verde and Porfido rosso. Although the conservation project is not yet complete, we are aware that the upper decorative zone cannot be completely attached to the walls because the pieces are too fragmented and the reconstruction is too uncertain. Therefore we are considering exhibiting the preserved panels in the Marble Hall.

The conservation project in the so-called Marble Hall (31) yielded numerous results reaching far beyond conservation studies. A detailed study of the stone processing and the mounting processes brought new discoveries about the craft of ancient building. The inscriptions discovered on the backs of the

Fig. 42: Opus sectile fragments of the wall revetment

slabs were not only indicative of the exact chronological classification of the marble decoration, but they are also an important source for the marble trade in the Roman Imperial period, for the building process in the Marble Hall itself and not least for questions of ownership in Terrace House 2.

Financed by the Ephesus-Foundation and the Borusan-Holding, both based in Istanbul, and scientifically supervised by the Austrian Archaeological Institute, the luxurious wall revetment of the Marble Hall of the Residential Unit 6 and the colorful wall paintings of the entire Terrace House 2 are not only supposed to be preserved but also give an impression of their original appearance.

The Chronology of Terrace House 2

Medusa mosaic in room 16a, residential unit 3

◀ Terrace House 2 from the north

The phases of building, decoration, use, and destruction can be traced separately in the case of Terrace House 2. A building phase describes the process in which the building is constructed or radically changed.

The decoration of the building can occur both directly following and because of a construction phase and also at a later point in time. While the building and decoration phases represent series of singular events, the use phase describes a process –the inhabitation by generations of people– that took place over a longer period of time. The end of a use phase is marked again by a renovation phase or by a destruction that can result in another building phase or in final abandonment.

Terrace House 2 was inhabited for about 250 years, beginning with its construction in the early 1st century AD up to its abandonment as a result of a large catastrophic earthquake around AD 270/280. A building life span of such length has left distinct traces in the archaeological record. Typically, only small renovations and repairs took place but sometimes changes in living style or extensive destruction led to a complete remodeling and furnishing of the houses. Such destructions were often used as an opportunity to realize new trends and respond to changes in taste. While mosaic floors often remained because of their durability, wall paintings were more frequently adapted to the changing trends. The walls are frequently covered by two or three layers of painted plaster, and in some cases eight layers were preserved. The abrupt destruction of AD 270/280 permits us to reconstruct the last phase of use: by linking architecture and furnishings associated with that level, the final environment of the inhabitants of Terrace House 2 may be reimagined.

Building Phase I (AD 25-50)
The construction of the apartment block dates to the Tiberian-Claudian period (around AD 25-50); however, older terrace walls, constructed in the Hellenistic period, were incorporated (*fig. 43*). In the first building phase, a total of six self-contained peristyle houses were constructed on three terraces. These peristyle houses are referred to as 'residential units' by archaeologists. While only small fragments remain of the wall painting, multiple mosaic floors can be attributed to this phase. A pavement with black and white decorative fields from the large formal room in residential unit 1 is a good example (SR 1/6); this room was later remodeled and developed into the so-called theater room (SR 6) (*fig.

Terrace House 2 was inhabited for about 250 years, beginning with its construction in the early 1st century AD up to its abandonment as a result of a large catastrophic earthquake around AD 270/280.

Fig. 43: Terrace House 2, building phase I

> *In the course of the 1ˢᵗ century AD, however, individual modifications and repairs as well as changes in the interior décor can be identified.*

44). These floors remained in use for about 250 years. In the course of the 1ˢᵗ century AD, however, individual modifications and repairs as well as changes in the interior décor can be identified. The majority of the residential units were later completely renovated with the exception of residential unit 2. This unit retained its layout from the imperial period without serious changes until its destruction in the 3ʳᵈ century AD.

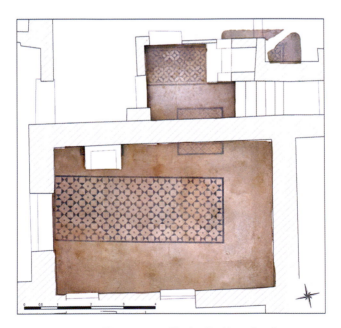

Fig. 44: Floor mosaic in SR 1/6 of building phase I

> *In the course of the necessary redecoration, its walls were covered with paintings on a red background, including the famous Socrates fresco which is now in the Efes Müzesi Selçuk.*

Building Phase II (around AD 120)

In the late Trajanic-Hadrianic period (AD 110-130), decisive changes to the building are noticeable (*fig. 45*). In residential unit 6, a large dining room, the so-called marble hall (31), was created by moving the south wall. The completely new design was remarkable in that the entire formal area was decorated with marble revetment. Moreover, the mounting of the revetment can be solidly dated due to the inscriptions on the back of the panels. According to these inscriptions, these changes to the structure cannot have been completed before AD 121. Around the same time, a bath was integrated into the eastern walkway of the peristyle courtyard (31a) with the room sequence of apodyterium (M3), tepidarium (M2) and caldarium (M1) that was heated by a praefurnium in the north-east of the walkway (31aNO). These renovations entailed the relocation of the entrance to residential unit 6 (31d).

Due to these renovations in residential unit 6, residential unit 4 lost its northern formal rooms (N1 and N2) (*fig. 46*). In the course of the necessary redecoration, its walls were covered with paintings on a red background, including the famous Socrates fresco which is now in the Efes Müzesi Selçuk (*fig. 47*). As late as building phase II, furthermore, residential

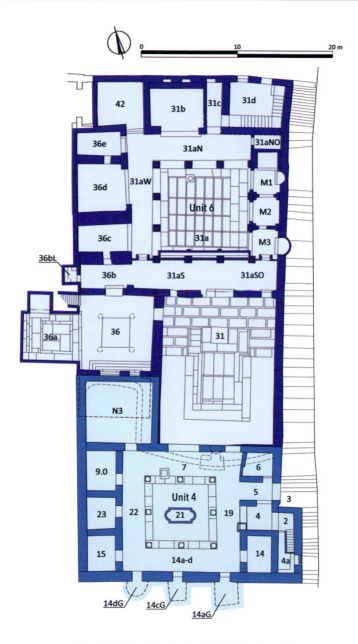

Fig. 45: Residential units 4 and 6, building phase II

Fig. 46: View of residential units 4 and 6

units 4 and 6 were architecturally and functionally joined.

Architectural renovations and new decorations can also be observed in residential unit 7

Fig. 47: The Socrates-fresco from residential unit 4

during building phase II. The columns of its large peristyle courtyard (38b) were renovated in the ground and second floors and the walls were also decorated with paintings on a red background, possibly showing a procession of gods. While the marble tile floor traces back to building phase I, the walkways of the peristyle were covered with a polychrome mosaic floor.

A bath was incorporated into the north end of the peristyle courtyard with a cold and warm bathing room (38e and 38h).

More renovations can be found in the second floor, where another smaller peristyle courtyard was created (32c/d); this would have been necessary for the accessibility of the upper stories as well as for lighting. Residential units 6 and 7 were already connected in building phase I and remained connected into phase II. In the other residential units, only small repairs and redecorations with new wall paintings can be identified. The construction of a private bath (SR 3) in residential unit 1 greatly compromised the building substance.

Building Phase III (around AD 150)
Around the mid-2nd century, residential unit 6 was again expanded with the construction of the so-called basilica –the large apsidal hall (8)– and smaller side rooms (*fig. 48*); of these side rooms, the stucco room (8a) is exceptional for its magnificent wall and ceiling décor. The courtyard (36) was also renovated, newly furnished, and in building phase III it was covered by a groin vault. The loss of this light source was made up for by the installation of oculi in the courtyard as well as in the adjoining vaulted room in the west

While the marble tile floor traces back to building phase I, the walkways of the peristyle were covered with a polychrome mosaic floor.

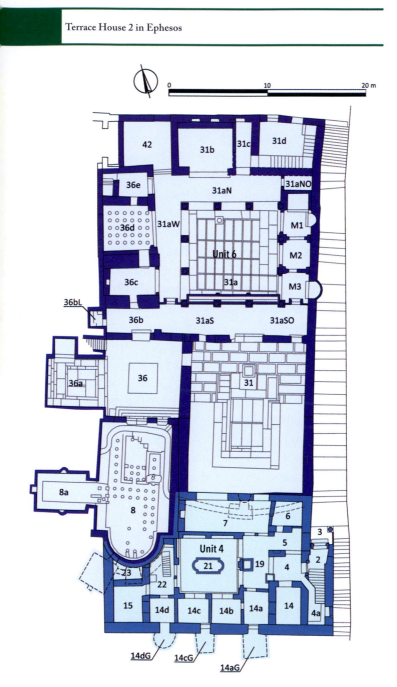

Fig. 48: Residential units 4 and 6, building phase III

(36a). Further renovations took place in the western rooms where room 36d was equiped with a hypocaust heating system that required a praefurnium. The heating systems of the recently constructed bath in the eastern walkway of the peristyle courtyard (31a) were also modified: a second praefurnium and tubuli were installed. The walls and floors were also newly decorated with marble tiles.

Fig. 49: The apsidal hall (8) in residential unit 6

Due to the southern expansion of residential unit 6 (*fig. 49*), the living space of residential units 4 and 5 –which adjoin unit 6 to the south and

The walls and floors were also newly decorated with marble tiles.

west– was diminished. The columns of the peristyle courtyard (21) of residential unit 4 were replaced by pillars of brick and the walkway was given up. While four approximately square rooms were created in the south (14a-d), an elongated room (7) was created in the north that overlooked the lower-laying marble hall (31) through a gallery. The loss of living space on the ground floor was compensated by the construction of a second floor.

During building phase III at the latest, residential units 3 and 5 were separated and residential unit 5 was entered through a long, narrow corridor from the west. Through the construction of an apsidal hall (8), the peristyle courtyard (24) had to be altered and its eastern walkway became narrower. The importance of the courtyard as a center of communication of the house was emphasized by the construction of a fountain ensemble and the addition of a formal room in the south (13). Residential unit 3 received another main room (12) and the northern, elongated room 17 that opens onto the peristyle courtyard (16b) was furnished with the lion mosaic. A building sacrifice was discovered under the threshold and dates this construction to the mid-2nd century AD (*fig. 50*).

In residential unit 7, only smaller architectural renovations took place during the building phase III though its walls were completely repainted.

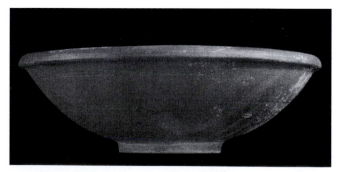

Fig. 50: A bowl used for a building sacrifice in residential unit 3

The archaeological record distinctly indicates a catastrophic destruction that can be dated to the late-Severan period (around AD 220/230) based on coins and pottery.

The monumental two-phase redesign of residential unit 6 into what has been called a 'city palace' was completed in building phase III and entirely changed the character of the insula. On the northern-most terrace of Terrace House 2, a public building complex of formal character was created that stood out among the adjoining private living quarters through its grouping of rooms, the meticulously planned architectural design, as well as its elaborate furnishings.

Building Phase IV (around AD 230)

The archaeological record distinctly indicates a catastrophic destruction (*fig. 51*) that can be dated to the late-Severan period (around AD 220/230) based on coins and pottery. This appears to have been caused by a severe earthquake or a series of earthquakes with subsequent fire. The latter interpretation is supported by the fact that the youngest wall painting and marble revetment in various rooms in Terrace House 2 was applied to clearly deformed and shifted walls. This is further supported by traces of repairs on columns, architraves and capitals that were reused in building phase IV. The finds amalgamated into the leveled surface partially feature heavy scorch marks; some objects have even been melted beyond recognition. Follow-

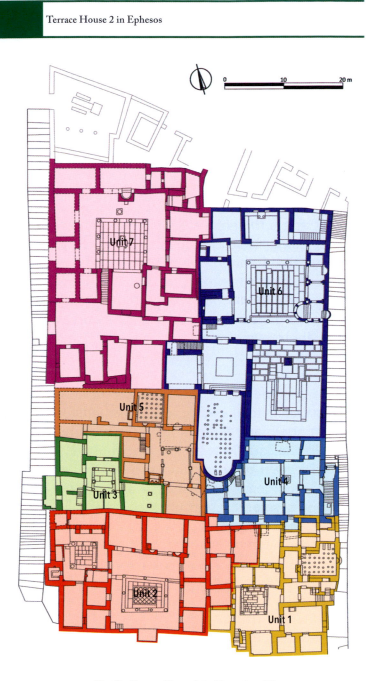

Fig. 51: Terrace House 2, building phase IV

ing the catastrophe, repairs and new furnishings can be identified in all of the residential units. The majority of the wall paintings as well as marble revetments dates to the second quarter of the 3rd century AD, while –as we have mentioned above– the older mosaic floors frequently remained in use.

Phase IV was the last large building and decorative phase, and as it was destroyed and sealed by debris, it is the phase that is the best known to archaeologists. The furnishings of each residential unit of this phase can be compared with each other since even the same craftsmen worked for different patrons in Terrace House 2. Because of this, differences in taste and also wealth are thus particularly apparent: although the decoration is similar, the character of each residential unit is unique. Considering the particular decoration and finds of the final phase, we can begin to access the final inhabitants. This is particularly the case when renovations, used objects, graffiti and also portraits can be connected with particular individuals and considered in tandem.

During phase IV, residential unit 1 lost four rooms to residential unit 2, which adjoined it in the west, and compensated for this loss of space

Although the decoration is similar, the character of each residential unit is unique.

To the south of the peristyle courtyard (SR 22/23), the vaulted room D, which had been cut out of bedrock, was added with its remarkable, eye-catching décor.

through the construction of small cubicula (SR 10a and SR 10b) north of the peristyle courtyard (SR 2). Furthermore, the entrance (SR 1) was moved so that a step leads from the higher lying stepped alley 1 into a courtyard (SR 1) with a decorative fountain. The bath of residential unit 1 (SR 3) had been so heavily destroyed (*fig. 52*) that the original hypocaust system was abandoned and filled up, and a new floor heating system was constructed at a higher level.

Residential unit 2 was not changed structurally, but expanded through the addition of

Fig. 52: The bathing room SR 3 of residential unit 1 in the decorative phase of the 3rd century AD

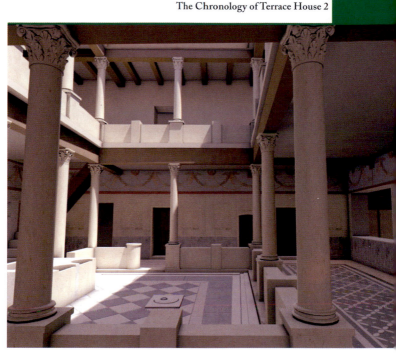

Fig. 53: Reconstruction of the peristyle courtyard SR 22/23

rooms in the east. Its complete redecoration – with mosaics, marble revetment and wall painting– is remarkable (*fig 53*). To the south of the peristyle courtyard (SR 22/23), the vaulted room D, which had been cut out of bedrock, was added with its striking, eye-catching décor.

The floor plans remained unaltered in residential units 3 and 5, but the elongated room to the south of the peristyle courtyard (16b) was divided into two smaller cubicula (16a). These new rooms were decorated with a magnificent mosaic floor that included figural decoration. In multiple rooms the walls were redecorated with paintings and marble slabs. The so-called Room of the Muses (12) of residential unit 3 is particularly remarkable because its paintings

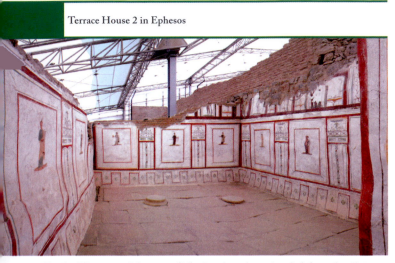

Fig. 54: The room of the muses (12) of residential unit 3 with deformed walls in the north

were applied to walls that had been severely deformed by an earthquake (*fig. 54*). Also in result of the seismic catastrophe, the arches in the courtyard (21) of residential unit 4 were closed. The decorative pool in the courtyard was abandoned and covered with a marble floor.

The appearance of the peristyle courtyard (31a) of residential unit 6 was completely altered and it received a columned hall in two of its upper stories. Thus, in the second quarter of the 3rd century AD, the courtyard had a total of three stories. At the same time the second floor was expanded while the third floor can only be reconstructed based on the courtyard architecture: the addition of this floor in the peristyle courtyard is the result of an architectural redesign of residential unit 6 that now extended across multiple levels. In the courtyard (31a), a small fountain was installed and the adjoining bath (M1-3) in the east was renovated. The apsidal hall (8) received a new floor heating system after the original water basin installed at floor level was given up and removed.

In residential unit 7, the heavily damaged columns of the peristyle courtyard (38b) were renovated and then reinstalled and the rooms were repaired and furnished with wall paintings and marble revetments. A connection to residential unit 6 cannot be definitively proven for this phase but could have existed: while the rooms in the east seem to have been accessible from residential unit 6, the small courtyard (32c/d) in the east of the upper story only provided access to the areas in the south, west and north.

Building Phase IV' (around AD 260)

The last verifiable building phase of Terrace House 2 is characterized by renovations that took place shortly before its final destruction and can therefore be dated to AD 260-270. This phase is the result of the earthquakes that increased in the course of the 3rd century and forced the inhabitants of Terrace House 2 to extensively renovate the structure and interior

This phase is the result of the earthquakes that increased in the course of the 3rd century and forced the inhabitants of Terrace House 2 to extensively renovate the structure and interior decoration.

Fig. 55: Revetment slabs prepared for reuse

decoration. The reconstruction of this event is particularly impressive in the so-called marble hall (31) in residential unit 6, where the marble revetment was being renovated at the time of the large catastrophe. The archaeological record suggests that the workmen were interrupted while they were working: finished panels ready to be mounted were lying on the floor of the hall when they were discovered by archaeologists while others were already fastened to the wall (*fig. 55*). This observation is probably also correct for the work on opus sectile panels of the uppermost decorative zone: a couple of these, including two with figural décor, were left lying almost undamaged on the floor. In addition, thousands of small pieces of debris, evidence of completed panels that had seemingly collapsed, as well as the location of dowels in the south wall are evidence that the workmen had already begun with the mounting of the opus sectile panels.

Due to its size, the marble hall also served as the workspace of craftsmen working on other renovations in residential unit 6. As a result additional marble slabs had been stacked against the walls, probably intended for the revetment of the courtyard (31a). Furthermore, there was a space for mixing mortar in an adjoining vaulted room (36a).

In residential unit 1, the collapse of a column in the peristyle (SR 2) and the resulting damage necessitated a renewal of the marble slab floor as well as the floor mosaic in the southern walkway. These repairs are still clearly visible. In residential unit 4, tools of craftsmen and masons were discovered that were left behind by workmen.

Further evidence for extensive renovations is the placement of some interior furnishings, not discovered in their original setting in the formal rooms but instead in side rooms, where they were placed temporarily. The busts of the emperor Marcus Aurelius (*fig. 56*) and a male private portrait

These repairs are still clearly visible. In residential unit 4, tools of craftsmen and masons were discovered that were left behind by workmen.

Fig. 56: Bust of emperor Marcus Aurelius, deposited in room 36a

are as unlikely to have been part of the original décor of the room 36a in residential unit 6 in which they were discovered; as a large blue glass slab, a statue of an Egyptian priest, a fitting of a kline, a folding chair and four-part collapsible legs of a table, all found in an inconspicuous side room (SR 12) of residential unit 2.

The Destruction (AD 270/280)

A catastrophe in the third quarter of the 3rd century (AD 270/280) led to the massive destruction of the insula (*fig. 57*). The archaeological record does not leave any doubt that this catastrophe was a heavy earthquake with subsequent fire that damaged the structure considerably and led to the abandonment of entire living areas. Extensive deformation, cracks, buckling and depression of the floors can best be seen in residential unit 7. The collapsed state of the columns and capitals as well as shifted, deformed and partially buckled walls illustrates the severity of the seismic catastrophe that ravaged Ephesos in the later Roman Imperial period. In result of the earthquake, a destructive fire broke out in Terrace House 2 and left behind scorched walls and masonry, house inventory melted be-

In many areas of Terrace House 2, the damage of earlier destructions was being removed and repairs taking place at the time of the catastrophe in AD 270/280.

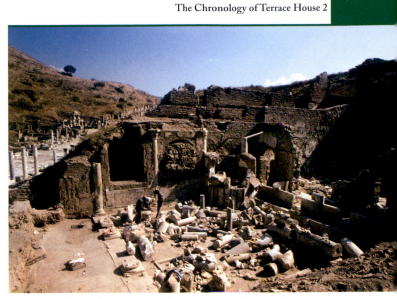

Fig. 57: The large peristyle courtyard 31a of residential unit 6

yond recognition, and charred wooden beams of the architraves, ceiling, and roof.

In many areas of Terrace House 2, the damage of earlier destructions was being removed and repairs taking place at the time of the catastrophe in AD 270/280. The residential units appear to have been largely uninhabited –aside from the groups of workmen– and this would explain the lack of human remains and the discovery of very little jewelry and few personal belongings. It is likely, however, that the debris was searched after the catastrophe and partially removed in order to rescue people buried under the collapse and to reach valuables.

Terrace House 2 from Late Antiquity to the Middle Ages

The insula in the heart of Ephesos did not remain uninhabited after the destruction. Further

Terrace House 2 in Ephesos

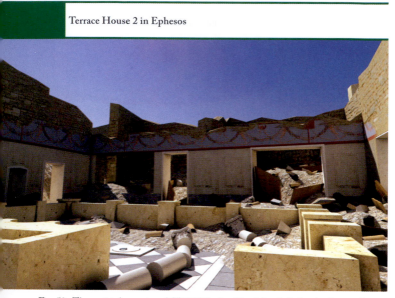

Fig. 58: The peristyle courtyard SR 22/23 of residential unit 2 after its destruction, 3D-reconstruction

uses and adaptations can be identified in all of its terraces. The initial renovations focused on the repair of sanitary facilities, particularly latrines. Moreover, individual adaptations to the changed circumstances are visible in each of the residential units after the catastrophe. In residential unit 1, individual rooms were walled off and filled with rubble while other areas of the apartment, such as the peristyle courtyard (SR 2), were used at the floor level of the Roman imperial period. In residential unit 2, the area to the west of the large peristyle courtyard (SR 22/23) as well as the small courtyard (SR 27), the latrine (SR 29), and possibly also single cubicula remained in use (*fig. 58*). In this case, the floor level of these later phases of use was frequently 1-1.5 meters higher than those of the imperial period. Above the levels of destruction, these simple floors were made of mud.

The situation in residential unit 7 is similar: on top of the rubble, walls were constructed that do not seem to follow any logical system. In the upper story of residential unit 7, the latrine (34/34a) was abandoned and the originally large room was divided into two connected, smaller units. This activity can be dated to the late 4th to early 5th century AD and illustrates the Late Antique building activity in the area of Terrace House 2.

In residential unit 6, the southern rooms as well as the peristyle courtyard (31a) remained buried, but the northern rooms (42 and 31b) as well as the former bath in the eastern walkway (M1-3) remained in use. It is interesting that the rooms were now connected with the tabernae in the north, while their entrances facing the peristyle court were walled off. The bath was abandoned, the basins filled with rubble and the marble furnishings removed. Its windows were also walled off and the room could only be accessed through the former stairway (31d). Possibly this had become a store room for the tabernae along the street; these were in use until the 7th century.

Along the western end of Terrace House 2, a mill complex was built in Late Antiquity

The latrine (34/34a) was abandoned and the originally large room was divided into two connected, smaller units.

The latest finds date to the period of the rulers of Aydın, who controlled Ephesos/Ayasoluk in the 14th century.

that was then expanded into a multi-functional workshop area in the early and middle Byzantine period (*fig. 59*). The older Roman walls were frequently reused, but the numerous Byzantine walls do not align with the imperial design. The oldest mill rooms in the north of Terrace House 2 were probably constructed in the 5th century, and the complex later expanded to the south in the 6th century AD. At the same time, a stone saw was put into operation where marble revetment slabs were cut and polished. Concentrations of metal finds, semi-finished products, and tools suggest the presence of metalworking workshops to the northwest of Terrace House 2. The accumulation of slag in the upper story of residential unit 7 is probably connected to these workshops. Byzantine buildings also developed in the area of residential unit 6, 3 meters above the Roman floor level, and exhibit sophisticated furnishing. Found above residential unit 1, a large building of the Byzantine period can be interpreted as a warehouse. In residential unit 2, it is unclear when the columns made of spolia with an overlying brick arch construction were built into the southern walkway of the peristyle courtyard (SR 22/23). They functioned as the substruc-

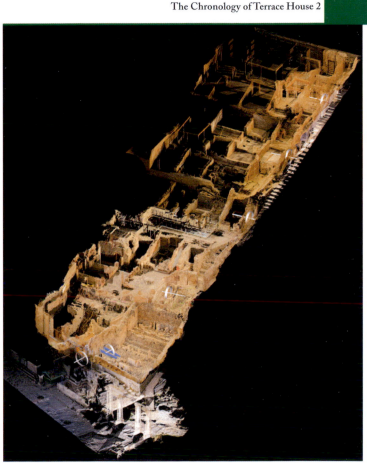

Fig. 59: Laser scan of the Byzantine line of mills above Terrace House 2

ture for the above-lying rooms that were in use until at least the early 7th century.

Based on the pottery finds, coins, and also later burials that were dug into the early Byzantine buildings, it can be shown that the area was still frequented in the middle and late Byzantine period. The latest finds date to the period of the rulers of Aydın, who controlled Ephesos/Ayasoluk in the 14th century.

Earlier Buildings under Terrace House 2

Hellenistic bowl with Asclepius and Hygieia from Terrace House 2

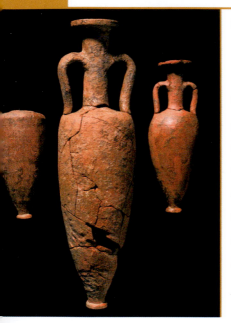

The geological subsurface of Terrace House 2 consists of green phyllites that can be found at the foot of the Bülbüldağ and that are mainly covered by the hillside debris of the Bülbüldağ.

Fig. 60: Late Classical amphoriskoi from graves under the Terrace House Street

Carbonate rocks occur above this disturbed geological zone. Phyllite is slate rock with a large amount of mica and is thus fairly soft and easily susceptible to weathering, but it is also easy to work. For a long time the hill functioned as a burial site. During excavations below the so-called Terrace House Street, burials in tile graves (*fig. 60*) were discovered that can be dated to the Late Classical period (first half of the 4th century BC) based on the grave goods. Scattered finds of Archaic and Classical pottery that are frequently found in the younger layers suggest the use of the area as a necropolis. The burial area lined the processional way of the goddess Artemis, which in the later Hellenistic period (2nd/1st century BC) was expanded

During excavations below the so-called Terrace House Street, burials in tile graves were discovered that can be dated to the Late Classical period (first half of the 4th century BC) based on the grave goods.

as an inner-urban boulevard, today referred to as Curetes Street.

In the late 3rd to early 2nd century BC, the slope was terraced (*fig. 61*). This can be associated with the Hellenistic development of the city and its reorganization. The massive, ashlar terrace walls made in this period continued to be in use in the Roman period and can still be seen in Terrace House 2. A narrow, west-east oriented street was discovered in deeper layers under the upper level of residential unit 7. However, since there is

Fig. 61: The Hellenistic terrace walls

Fig. 62: A Hellenistic oven

a 100-year gap between the construction of the street and the first verifiable and datable structures, it is unknown whether buildings were immediately constructed on these terraces. Regardless, by the 2nd century BC at the latest, workshop areas developed on all three terraces.

The number of ovens is surprisingly high (*fig. 62*) and they correspond to the type still used in the Middle East, the tannur. The excellent preservation of some of the ovens in Terrace House 2 makes it possible to reconstruct them precisely: on a carefully laid tile floor, round, clay walls were molded up to 6 cm thick. Through the first use of the oven, the oven wall –clay combined with rich inclusions of organic material– was fired; in this process, the plant remains carbonized and created cavities that heightened the oven's capacity for heat storage. Most of the examples in Terrace House 2 had closed walls without an opening at the bottom for stoking the fire. An opening must have, therefore, been located off center and higher or also centrally in the dome. Tannurs are primarily used for baking flat bread but they are also all-purpose ovens with a variety of primary and secondary functions. In Terrace House 2, archaeologists have determined that these ovens were used to fire pottery; to do so, the floor of the oven was covered with brushwood or dried dung, then unfired but dry vessels were placed on top of the fuel and the fire was lit. The necessary firing temperature of 600-800°C could be reached without problem. The rows of ovens under residential units 1 and 2 were set within a web of walls and canals that likely defined a large, commercial area. Their reconstruction is not possible due to the later construction that cut into the older, lower layers.

Deep wells were cut into the bedrock of all three terraces to secure the water supply of the area. The geological subsurface was ideal for this purpose because the easily pliable phyllite has the capability of accumulating water. The majority of these wells remained in use after the construction of the Roman

The number of ovens is surprisingly high and they correspond to the type still used in the Middle East, the tannur.

Fig. 63: Hellenistic wall paintings from houses under Terrace House 2

A Hellenistic fountain house, still visible to the right of the entrance to Terrace House 2, is one of the oldest-standing monuments that now line the street.

apartments. The commercial zone extended across the entire western half of Terrace House 2 to residential unit 7 located in the northwest, where another tannur is still visible in the north walkway of the peristyle courtyard (38b).

The archaeological discoveries under residential unit 6 are completely different from those described above. In the area of the later peristyle courtyard (31a), a smaller inner courtyard was discovered, furnished with polished mosaic floors and other rooms decorated with mosaics that suggest a late Hellenistic private house. The high-quality wall painting fragments (*fig. 63*) that were leveled after the house was abandoned can be divided into two phases. The older paintings, indicating when the Hellenistic house was constructed, date to the late 2nd or early 1st century BC. Later painting fragments from the second half of the 1st century BC probably belong to the last decorative phase of the Hellenistic house, before the building was razed for the construction of the Roman insula. As a result, the length of use of the late Hellenistic house complex probably took place between 100 BC-AD 25/50.

In the Hellenistic period, the northern end of the area was already marked by a row of tabernae that open up onto the Curetes Street, which was not yet paved with marble but instead was a packed gravel path. A Hellenistic fountain house (*fig. 64*), still visible to the right of the entrance to Terrace House 2, is one of the oldest-standing monuments that now line the street. The so-called Heroon of Androcles was probably built in the first half of the 1st century BC; this was followed by the Octagon in the last decades BC.

Fig. 64: Lion spout from the Hellenistic fountain house north of Terrace House 2

Living in
Terrace House 2

Bust of the emperor Marcus Aurelius

◀ Statuette of Athena

Terrace House 2 in Ephesos

Fig. 65: The entrance to residential unit 4

General Characteristics of the Residential Units

According to the original early imperial design, the six comparably-sized residential units were large peristyle houses (400-600 m²) that stretched across three terraces and had at least one upper floor.

During the almost 300-year-long period of use, the houses were frequently renovated, drastically changed from their original state. The house on the central terrace, for example, was divided up between residential units 3 and 5 in the course of the 2nd century, and through expansion and formal decoration, residential unit 6 developed into a city palace.

The main entrances to the houses were mainly situated along the narrow stepped alleys and were partially emphasized through the marble revetment of the portals (*fig. 65*). According to the typology of the floor plans, two variations of peristyle houses can be dif-

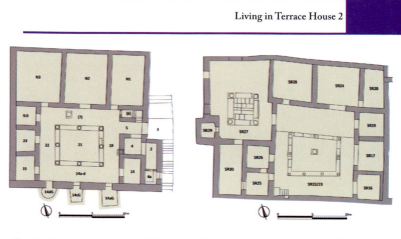

Fig. 66: Residential unit 4 in building phase I

Fig. 67: Residential unit 2 in building phase I

ferentiated in the first building phase of Terrace House 2. The first type is characterized by a central, columned courtyard (*fig. 66*) that was entered through a narrow foyer. The courtyard was surrounded by a walkway that led to other rooms of the house. The second type retained the central peristyle with surrounding columned hall (*fig. 67*), but another courtyard was set in front of it that functioned as the entrance and point from which side and domestic rooms could be entered.

The central peristyle courtyard functioned as the distribution room, communication cent-

The main entrances to the houses were mainly situated along the narrow stepped alleys and were partially emphasized through the marble revetment of the portals.

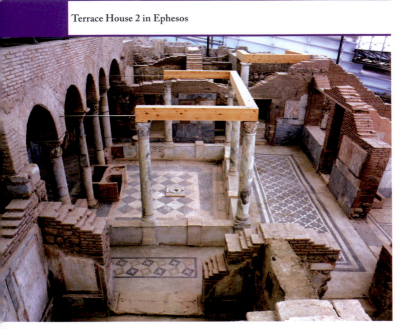

Fig. 68: The peristyle courtyard SR 22/23 of residential unit 2

er and formal reception room for guests and clients (*fig. 68*). This center and heart of the house was elaborately decorated with carefully-chiseled blocks and wall revetments of marble or other colored stones, high-quality wall paintings, multi-colored mosaic floors and decorative fountains. The collection and decorative mounting of reliefs and three-dimensional works of art emphasized the importance of the columned courtyard as the representative heart of the house. These open courtyards had the additional and very important function of supplying lighting and ventilation. The furnishings for the house cult were situated in the entrance areas as well as the courtyards. Of course, these spaces were arranged differently according to the circumstances, preferences and traditions of the household. Numerous small nich-

At the southern end of the house were rooms or groups of rooms that were particularly important because of their prominent position and costly furnishings.

es held the heroes and funeral banquet reliefs, and individual rooms were designated for the performance of ritual.

At the southern end of the house were rooms or groups of rooms that were particularly important because of their prominent position and costly furnishings (*fig. 69*). These rooms can be identified as reception and waiting rooms. Also in the southern end, small rooms used for the storage and cooling of food were hewn into the bedrock, taking full advantage of the location of the houses on the slope. In the north end of the house, large formal rooms accommodated convivial symposia. These northern

Fig. 69: The exedra in residential unit 1

In accordance with the superior standard of living of the inhabitants, the houses were equipped with heated rooms and bathrooms.

rooms, impressive with their ornate furnishings and decoration, were usually linked with the courtyards through wide door openings or windows. Additional rooms with expensive furnishings were often located across from the entrance area directly adjoining the courtyards. They were intended to be noticed by those first entering.

Besides these main rooms, numerous other side rooms, cubicula, and cellae also existed; they could be entered either through the courtyard walkway or through other rooms. Their simple furnishings as well as subordinate location within the house design mark them as different from the other rooms and they indicate their function as sleeping or resting rooms. In the Roman world, children did not receive their own space; children of the owners either slept with their parents or their nurses. The servants were put up in the courtyards and workrooms. The areas used for kitchens, other household work, and latrines were mainly located in the entrance areas and could in fact be used by multiple residential units. In accordance with the superior standard of living of the inhabitants, the houses were equipped with heated rooms and bathrooms.

Building Materials

In the course of the terracing work the subsurface of mica-slate was hewn in order to create flat surfaces so that buildings could be constructed. During the construction of the Hellenistic terrace walls, local limestone breccia was broken into large ashlar blocks and carefully set without mortar. The rising walls of the Roman insula were made of quarry stones and bricks. Generally, quarry stone and bricklaying techniques occurred concurrently throughout all the building phases, but the use of brick walls became more prominent in the 3rd century AD. The majority of the walls from building phase I (AD 25-50) were constructed with quarry stones and mortar. The stones –of local, gray-blue marble– originated from nearby, partially inner-urban quarries that can still be found on the Panayırdağ. Other quarry stones of limestone-breccia as well as marble spolia are also used in the walls of the initial construction of Terrace House 2. Bricks were preferred for arch and vault construction, but it is apparent that these techniques became a popular architectural feature only after building phase II. After building phase II (around AD 120), opus mixtum walls, characterized by alternating quarry stones and brick layers, appeared. It is surprising that during the repair and renovation measures shortly before the final earthquake catastrophe (building phase IV', around AD 260), dried mudbricks were again used prominently as building materials. At this time, thin slabs of mica-slate were added as leveling courses in the quarry stone walls, and these can also

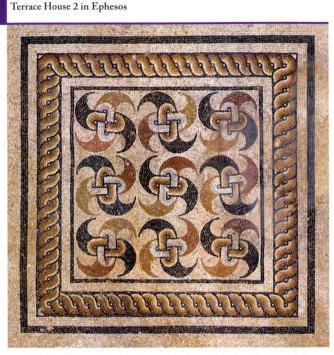

Fig. 70: The multi-colored mosaic in the exedra of residential unit 1

be found as covers of canals. Due to the high thermal conductivity of the material, it was also used in the area of praefurnia and hypocausts.

Floor pavements could be made with a variety of materials, including simple mud or mortar, mosaic, and marble and brick slabs. Mortar floor pavements were quite rare and usually only functioned as the bedding for a more decorative pavement. An example of this is with the so-called opus signinum technique found in residential unit 6; the smooth surface of the polished floor mosaic guaranteed that it was waterproof. Mud floor pavements were more common and are usually found in side rooms. It is possible that the packed mud served only as a foundation for wooden floors, now lost and so not verifiable. Large-format brick tiles were also used as a floor covering, though infrequently; in the so-called room of the muses (12) of residential unit 3, the tiles stand in stark contrast to elaborate wall decoration.

Mosaic floors were used a lot more frequently, prized for being waterproof and low-maintenance, among other things (*fig. 70*). Before a mosaic floor was installed, a layer of gravel was set to avoid unevenness. During the installation, the little small pieces of colored stone were set into a bed of mortar; after the floor was completely laid fine grout was spread across the surface to fill the gaps. The black tesserae are dolomite and volcanic rock; the white tesserae as well as the red ones are limestone, while oolitic lime or a fine-grained dolomite were used for yellow. The production of glass tesserae with inlaid gold foil was particularly intricate and expensive, and thus done very rarely. An exceptionally luxurious variation of glass mosaic sometimes was used to decorate walls and also vaulting. The glass material allowed for a more nuanced, colorful radiance, especially as it caught the light, and this greatly heightened the plasticity and effect of the images depicted by the mosaic.

Mosaic floors were used a lot more frequently, prized for being waterproof and low-maintenance, among other things.

120

Bases, columns, capitals, parapets and carefully-chiseled blocks were made of marble, and to a lesser extent granite and limestone. Traces of the white coating of lime sludge indicate that many architectural elements were originally stuccoed and possibly also painted. Many furnishings, including furniture and decorative elements, were also constructed out of marble. The abundant –seemingly wasteful– use of marble was possible due to the rich deposits in the surroundings of Ephesos. Numerous quarries in the hinterland and along the

Ephesian marble was also an important commodity that was exported via the harbor of the city.

Fig. 71: Marble slab floor in the peristyle courtyard 31a of residential unit 6

Fig. 72: Opus sectile floor in the exedra of residential unit 2

coast supplied the city with high-quality white marble. Ephesian marble was also an important commodity that was exported via the harbor of the city: the Ephesian Greco Scritto, for example, can be found throughout the Roman Empire. Marble was also a material commonly used for the revetment of walls and floors. The laying of marble slab floors (*fig. 71*) could have demonstrated status as well as had practical reasons. For example, the peristyle courtyard (31) and also the dining or audience hall (8) of residential unit 6 were furnished with marble, but at the same time, marble floors were common in bathing rooms, surrounding fountains, as well as in latrines. A specific variation of marble revetment was opus sectile flooring (*fig. 72*) that is extremely rare in Terrace House 2. For its production, marble and colored slabs were polished, cut, and then assembled into decorative patterns or fields on the floor. To date, opus sectile floors have only been discovered in the second story of residential unit

Walls without marble revetment were either simply plastered or decorated with wall painting.

Fig. 73: A typical marble revetment of a wall in Terrace House 2

4 and in the exedra (GEW D) of residential unit 2; it seems that this form of floor decoration did not become popular until Late Antiquity.

In contrast, the revetment of walls with marble and colored stone was particularly common in Terrace House 2 (*fig. 73*). The mounting of the slabs required a mortar filling 4 cm thick, made of lime, sand, brick dust and also mica and brick chippings. The slabs were also attached using dowels and small bronze hooks. The surface was polished after the mounting was completed. The fountains of Terrace House 2 were also typically revetted with marble slabs embellished with a decorative zone of mosaic or opus sectile. The most noteworthy example of this is probably the upper decorative zone in the marble hall (31) of residential unit 6. The use of a variety of stones enhanced the color of the decoration, accented the form of the fountain, and emphasized the wealth and social status of its owners. No cost and efforts were spared in order to acquire prestigious and expensive marbles and colored stone from various regions of the Roman Empire and bring them to Ephesos. The list of the varieties of stone is long and includes such well-known types as cipollino verde, pavonazzetto, rosso brecciato, verde antico, africano nero, bigio antico, porfido rosso, giallo antico, rosso antico, alabastro fiorito, and last but not least, proconnesian marble.

Walls without marble revetment were either simply plastered or decorated with wall painting (*fig. 74*). Depending on the importance and function of the room, the walls could be covered with a rough or fine plaster of lime mortar with mica slate grit as an additive. The walls and the less frequent ceilings that were to be painted in a fresco technique were plastered especially carefully. The 1-3 cm thick rough plaster was first covered by a 1-2 mm thin coat of lime (or gymsum) and marble dust. While still wet, this surface was painted with

Fig. 74: The god Apollo Musagetes from the room of the muses (12) in residential unit 3

colors. The pigment and mortar fused together in the process of drying and formed a permanent bond, becoming extremely durable and stable. The colors were produced out of a mixture of fine pigments and lime and the rich palette ranged from ochre pigments and jarosite and green earth to the best known pigment of antiquity, Egyptian blue.

A favorite wall and ceiling embellishment was white or painted stucco (*fig. 75*) that included simple, often plain imitations of marble slabs but also elaborate and highly artistic molded designs. There are many examples of stucco molding in the Terrace House: in residential unit 2, for example, the stuccoed and painted walls of a room (SR 17) imitate a multi-zoned marble revetment. The masterpiece of this trade is without a doubt the stucco room (8a) of resi-

Fig. 75: A marble imitation stucco décor from SR 17

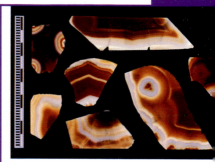

Fig. 76: Fragments of agate panes

In Terrace House 2, two iron window grates were discovered that were originally closed with glass windowpanes.

dential unit 6, where the vault and lunette were luxuriously decorated with highly molded stucco.

Evidence for window glass is only limited to the mentions in diaries of past archaeologists, very few preserved fragments, and of course the 'negative impression', i.e., the window frames found in the buildings. In Terrace House 2, two iron window grates were discovered that were originally closed with glass windowpanes. Windows in wooden frames appear to have been common in all the residential units. They were especially prevalent for the lighting in areas adjoining courtyards and to store heat in bathing facilities. For the production of the windowpanes, the light-blue-green to colorless and very transparent raw material was blown into cylinders, cut open and laid out. This technique produced highly transparent glass and increased the light permeability. Luxurious decorative windows also existed that were inlayed with very thinly cut slices of agate (*fig. 76*) or alabaster panes, and thus produced impressive lighting effects.

Nails, brackets, hooks and dowels –mostly iron, seldom bronze– had many different uses during house construction.

Fig. 77: A dowel in the wall

Metals were mainly used as connecting elements for wood or hewn stone constructions. Nails, brackets, hooks and dowels –mostly iron, seldom bronze– had many different uses during house construction (*fig. 77*). The existence of iron window grates has already been mentioned above; in addition, door hinges, locks, locking mechanisms, and numerous fittings of doors and parts of furniture were made of metal. Lead, another important material, was used for the ascending water pipes of the fountains, among other things.

The importance of brick as the building material for walls and as floor covering has already been mentioned. Moreover, the hypocaust pillars (pilae) for the floor heating were constructed with round and square tiles (*fig. 78*). Special forms were hollow tiles (tubuli) (*fig. 79*) and tegulae mammatae (*fig. 80*), both types mounted onto the walls as heat conductors.

Fig. 78: Hypocaust pillars in room 26 of residential unit 5

Clay water pipes were used for the supply of water and drainage of waste water (*fig. 81*), and sometimes for the escape of heat in baths and kitchens.

Finally, we must turn to wood, one of the most important and widespread building materials only seldom preserved in the archaeological record. This material was used in a variety of ways,

Fig. 79: Hollow tile, tubuli, carefully placed along the walls

Fig. 80: Tegula mammata

Fig. 81: A sewer pipe

including scaffolding, ceiling or ring beams, suspended ceilings, wall anchors, doors and lintels and also as floor coverings. Wood can be deduced from negative findings, i.e. impressions or cavities (*fig. 82*), such as beam and scaffolding holes or beam abutments on coping. Wickerwork or wattle was employed for narrower walls and lighter suspended ceilings. The diaries of previous archaeologists mention charred wooden beams and charcoal layers discovered in Terrace House 2; these probably orig-

Wickerwork or wattle was employed for narrower walls and lighter suspended ceilings.

inated from the ceiling and roof construction. Wooden elements were sometimes elaborately decorated, as can be seen in the marble hall (31) of residential unit 6, where the wooden beam ceiling was once covered with lavish wood carving clad with gold foil. The wood craft played an important role in the construction of the houses although very little of it is still preserved. Doors, window frames, and shutters have already been mentioned, but most furniture –tables, chairs, klinai, chests, cupboards, shelves and much more– was made either entirely or partially of wood. The objects of daily use, such as tools and components of dishes, also should not be overlooked, despite the fact that they were made of ephemeral materials.

Fig. 82: Beam holes above the wall painting zone in peristyle courtyard SR 22/23

Multi-Level Architecture

All of the residential units included an upper story; in the cases of residential units 4 and 6, a third story has been confirmed for at least the last phase of use (around AD 260). Due to structural issues it is reasonable to assume that the floor plans of the upper stories largely corresponded to those of the ground floor. The various floor levels could be reached via stairs in the courtyards and vestibules, but some also had separate entrances to the upper floors (*fig. 83*). Such a situation has been demonstrated, for example, in residential unit 4, where a staircase parallel to stepped alley 1 allowed access to the second floor. This was also the case for residential unit 7, as its upper story could be reached via stepped alley 3. The ground and

Fig. 83: The staircase to the second floor in residential unit 4

> *The various floor levels could be reached via stairs in the courtyards and vestibules, but some also had separate entrances to the upper floors.*

second floors thus did not have to be directly connected, or inhabited by the same family. It can be argued, for example, that the second floor of residential unit 1 was rented out; this is indicated by the recess for the socket of the hinges in the jointly-used vestibule, suggesting that the living areas could each be locked individually. It is possible that shops with street access were located in the second floors, and thus did not need to be connected with the house.

The furnishings and inventory of the ground floors have mainly been preserved *in situ* or in their collapsed position while the reconstruction of the upper stories relies on the find material from the debris (*fig. 84*). It is clear, however, that the rich furnishings of the upper-story apartments were remarkable and at times even more extravagant than those of the ground floor. For example, room 36d.1 of residential unit 6 was furnished with an artistically impressive mosaic floor, a cascading fountain and a heating system. The upper stories also contained spaces to accommodate all of the activities necessary in a noble household. These included the formal areas including columned courtyards, porticos, triclinia and partially heated cubicula, as well as industrial areas or latrines, kitchens and small

Terrace House 2 in Ephesos

The engraved inscription of an apparently content visitor is certain proof that guests were received, wined and dined in the upper floors.

Fig. 84: Reconstruction of the 3-story residential unit 4

courtyards. Expensive marble decoration, mosaic and opus sectile floors, figural wall painting, decorative fountains, and luxurious furniture speak to an intention for the interior space to have an external impact. The engraved inscription of an apparently content visitor is certain proof that guests were received, wined and dined in the upper floors.

An unusual aspect of Terrace House 2 is that individual residential units were connected and that they shared certain areas, including especially the more functional household areas such as latrines, and also water supply. As a rule, it was possible to pass from one upper story into that of the next house. The attraction of the upper stories might also have been based on the possibility of terraces and exterior windows, which would have offered an impressive view of the city of Ephesos and its surroundings.

Lighting and Ventilation

The natural lighting and ventilation of the houses, particularly of the ground level, was achieved through the central, open peristyle. This was supplemented by windows that were frequently placed above the doors (*fig. 85*), and of course also by the door openings themselves, which supported good ventilation. By

Fig. 85: A high window above a door to the apsidal room (8) of residential unit 6

'windows' we should differentiate between those that communicated to the outside world and interior windows. Large, glass interior windows set into wooden frames separated the peristyle

Fig. 86: Window between the peristyle courtyard (38b) and the adjoining rooms in residential unit 7

Fig. 87: An iron window grate

Round ceiling windows (oculi) were placed in vaulted rooms to aid lighting and could be closed up with tiles as necessary.

courtyard of residential units 2 (SR 22/23) and 7 (38b) from adjoining formal rooms (*fig. 86*). Interior windows were also placed between residential units. A glass window grate connected the room of the muses (12) of residential unit 3 with the formal room (13) of the adjoining residential unit 5 (*fig. 87*). Round ceiling windows (oculi) were placed in vaulted rooms to aid lighting and could be closed up with tiles

Fig. 88: Reconstruction of the windows in the marble hall (31) of the residential unit 6

as necessary. We can also guess that the bathing rooms were furnished with arched windows of glass.

A sophisticated lighting design was installed in the large staterooms in the south of residential unit 6 in the mid-2nd century AD (*fig. 88*). Light entered the marble hall (31) through windows with folding shutters that opened up to the adjoining peristyle courtyard (31a) in the north, to stepped alley 1 in the east, and to the interior courtyard of room 36 in the west. The apsidal hall (8)

Fig. 89: A Roman lamp of clay

received its light through a large, arched window that filled the entire lunette of the north wall; in contrast, the luxuriously decorated stucco room (8a) was only indirectly lighted by a skylight.

The rooms in the upper stories were probably better lighted and airier than those on the ground floor due to the possibility of exterior windows.

Additional lighting was provided from lamps made of clay (*fig. 89*), metal (*fig. 90*), and sometimes also glass, but the open fire was a constant fire hazard. Long, decorated, bronze candle holders in which lamps could be mounted, so-called candela-

Fig. 90: A Roman bronze lamp

bras, have also been preserved. Further lighting materials included kindling, torches and candles of organic –and thus not preserved– materials.

A comfortable room climate was enhanced by potted plants that were mainly set up in the courtyards. It is also possible that vegetables, herbs and spices were grown in the household courtyards.

The most impressive in this context is without doubt the apsidal hall (8) in residential unit 6, and also the adjoining stucco room (8a) to the west.

Room Ceilings and the Roofscape

Many of the rooms in Terrace House 2, including the numerous walkways of the peristyle courtyards, had wooden beam ceilings of which remain charcoaled wood fragments and now empty holes for the beams. These ceilings were either completely visible or their undersides were covered with plaster and paint. Remains of ceiling paintings from residential unit 2 (SR 19/20 and SR 24) and 3 (12) had a substructure of especially light wickerwork (*fig. 91*). Particularly for stately rooms, a ceiling of decorated wooden coffers can be assumed. A very elaborate example for this can be found in the marble hall (31) of residential unit 6, where the wooden beams were covered with carvings and gilding depicting sea creatures (*fig. 92*).

Vaulted ceilings made of brick have been documented since building phase I (AD 25-

Fig. 91: Fragment of ceiling paintings with wicker impression

50) and could take the form of barrel vaults, groin vaults, or corner arc arches, which was preferred for flights of stairs. The preferred design in construction was the barrel vault (*fig. 93*), which appears in formal, main rooms but also in baths, heating rooms, latrines and storage areas. The most impressive in this context is without doubt the apsidal hall (8) in residential unit 6, and also the adjoining stucco room (8a) to the west. The bathing rooms (M1-2) in the eastern walkway in the peristyle courtyard (31a) of residential unit 6 have a flat dome vault (*fig. 94*) that was built in building phase IV (around AD 230).

Fig. 92: A charred wooden beam of the ceiling of the marble hall (31) of residential unit 6

Fig. 93: The vaulted ceiling in the stucco room (8a) of residential unit 6

An excellent example of a groin vault with an oculus or opaion, has been partially preserved in room 36 of residential unit 6. Comparable oculi can be seen in the barrel vaulted rooms 36a and 38c.

A definitive reconstruction of the original roof of Terrace House 2 is not possible, but we can assume that it was uneven, made up of smaller surfaces which made the roofscape appear quite varied (*fig. 95*). The roof

Fig. 94: The flat vaulted dome in bath (M1-2) of residential unit 6

The roofs were centered on the open courtyards; their columned walkways were covered by roofs slanted inwards, draining the water at an angle of 15-20° into the courtyard.

tiles (tegulae and imbrices) were mounted on a supportive wooden framework. The roofs were centered on the open courtyards; their columned walkways were covered by roofs slanted inwards, draining the water at an angle of 15-20° into the courtyard. In other cases, downspouts diverted the water into canals under Terrace House 2 to the stepped alleys. Flat roofs are only seldom identified and were generally converted into terraces.

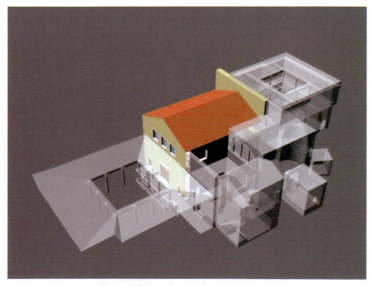

Fig. 95: The roofscape of residential unit 6

Fountains and Latrines

Deep wells are present on all three levels of Terrace House 2 for drawing ground water; these were constructed in the Hellenistic period, long before the construction of the insula. The round well shafts have a diameter of about 1 m, and while their upper part was usually made of a circle of stone blocks, the deeper part was hewn out of the bedrock. The wells, up to 18 m deep, could be covered with tiles, though in particular cases a decorative wellhead was verified, such as a 1st century BC relief of a nymph in residential unit 4. The Hellenistic construction is further accented by puteal wellheads, as can still be seen in residential unit 7 (*fig. 96*). The wells remained in use even after Terrace House 2 was connected to long-distance water pipes, as discussed below, and must have provided drinking water during droughts.

In building phase II, around AD 120, Terrace House 2 was connected

Fig. 96: A deep well with puteal wellhead

Deep wells are present on all three levels of Terrace House 2 for drawing ground water.

to a 40-km-long water pipe system, the Değirmendere aqueduct; arriving from the south, it supplied entire city quarters with drinking water. Since the insula was set on a slope, its upper stories could be connected to the water network without complicated pump systems and so fountains, baths and latrines could be installed there – this was different from Roman houses in flat areas. The supply pipes ran through the stepped alleys where the pipes were installed between the road surface and the arches of the sewer canals (*fig. 97*). The supply pipes installed in walls or un-

Fig. 97: The stepped alley 3 with water facilities

der floors were generally made of clay; the pipes ascending to fountains were made of lead (*fig. 98*), and distribution boxes made it possible for these pipes to supply multiple fountains at the same time. Addi-

Fig. 98: Lead pipes

Fig. 99: A built sewer canal

tionally, as mentioned above, rainwater was collected over the roofs in the courtyards. Below the floors of the houses is an extensive and complex web of water supply pipes and sewer canals. These canals (*fig. 99*) transported the rainwater and waste to the canals under the stepped alleys, which then led to the main canal under the Curetes Street.

The water fountains were mainly situated in the entrance areas and the courtyards of houses, and were thus easily accessible for the inhabitants, the owners and servants, and also the guests. Fountains are also often found in dining rooms and, of course, in baths. They varied in size and decoration depending on their location, and as a result also in their function: their forms range from simple square box fountains in the household areas (*fig. 100*) to multi-piece nymphaea with marble and glass mosaic decoration in the more formal rooms. The water piped up through lead pipes gushed into one or multiple basins; a hole in the basin wall prevented it from overflowing and let excess water drain into sewer canals. Water faucets of bronze regulated the constant stream of water.

Magnificently decorated fountains with a constant flow of water, decorative water basins, and fountain figures would have been

Water faucets of bronze regulated the constant stream of water.

Fig. 100: A box fountain in residential unit 2

appreciated both visually and acoustically, and thus greatly contributed to the atmosphere of a room. The function of a fountain arrangement, directly representative of the status of its owner, was enhanced by the sophistication of its design of cascades and spray, but also through the use of very expensive materials.

In the western walkway of the peristyle courtyard (24) of residential unit 5, an elabo-

Fig. 101: A niche fountain in residential unit 5

Fig. 102: A jet fountain in the marble hall (31) in residential unit 6

rately designed fountain ensemble (*fig. 101*) was constructed in building phase III, around AD 150. The fountain, with a back wall structured by three niches flanked by delicate columned architecture, occupies the entire width of the porticus. The elongated rectangular main basin is situated in front of the niches; an overflow basin is located on the eastern narrow side. Another niche fountain is connected to the display and its half-dome is revetted with an opus sectile surface of contrasting color.

Particularly spectacular, and also constructed in building phase III, was the jet fountain in the marble hall (31) of residential unit 6 (*fig. 102*); built in the center of the northern part of the room, this jewel was decorated with alabaster; and also had a central water outlet for a fountain. A fluted basin stand holding a ribbed shell of marble completed the artistic arrangement.

All of the houses of Terrace House 2 also had multiple toilets, so-called latrines (*fig. 103*). They were located in the entrance areas or the courtyards, often close to fountains, and they have also been proven to have existed in

All of the houses of Terrace House 2 also had multiple toilets, so-called latrines.

Fig. 103: The latrine (SR 29) in residential unit 2

the upper stories. Most latrines could accommodate multiple people at the same time. Numerous etched inscriptions in the toilets illustrate that the visit to the latrines was a social event –even in the private sphere– and that sometimes people remained longer than necessary. It is not surprising, therefore, that the latrines in the guest areas were elaborately furnished. An impressive example is the latrine (36bL) in residential unit 6, built around AD 120 in building phase II, decorated with marble wall revetment and floor.

Frequently coins are found in latrine canals that probably were lost during the visit to the toilet. People sat on built brick benches with openings through which the excrement fell into the canal. A continuous stream of water and the connection with the canal guaranteed high hygienic standards and very little offensive smell. Sponges mounted on wooden sticks were used to clean the buttocks; additionally, water flowing in gutters along the latrine benches could be used for cleaning purposes.

Often additional flushing was necessary, as evidenced by jugs discovered in the latrines.

Bathing and Heating

Many rooms in Terrace House 2 had a floor heating system (hypocaust). When determining the function of rooms it is important to differentiate between bathing rooms and heated warm rooms. The firing of the heating system took place outside the rooms in firing chambers (praefurnium), from which the hot air was conducted through the floors into the rooms (*fig. 104*). The floors and walls were heat conductors and were frequently also revetted with materials that stored heat. The installation of warm rooms in Terrace House 2 became more common in building phase III, around AD 150, and this phenomenon could be associated with a climate change.

The rooms that can be identified as prominent common rooms or even as winter triclinia, such as room 26 in residential unit 5 or room 36d in residential unit 6, were affected by this building activity. In the second quarter of the 3rd century, a hypocaust floor was added in the large apsidal hall (8) of residential unit 6 and the room was heated through a praefurnium to its south.

Fig. 104: Praefurnium and testudo in the bath (SR 3) of residential unit 1

Fig. 105: Hypocaust and tub in the bath (SR 3) of residential unit 1

The construction of multiple baths in Terrace House 2 can be linked to the availability of a long-distance water supply after about AD 120 and the consequent effortless access to larger quantities of water. In residential units 6 and 7, multi-room bathing facilities were built that included the paradigmatic elements of Roman bathing culture: the cold, warm and hot bath (frigidarium, tepidarium, caldarium) as well as probably a small sweat bath (sudatorium). This way the family as well as their guests were given the option of bathing in a small bath instead of visiting a large public bathing complex. Large basins used for cleansing and personal hygiene were elaborately decorated with marble revetment,

Many rooms in Terrace House 2 had a floor heating system (hypocaust).

Fig. 106: Bathing basin in residential unit 6

Because of its spatial separation from residential unit 1, the area could have possibly even been rented out and thus used by external individuals.

glass mosaics and stucco (*fig. 106*). In residential unit 1, bathing room SR 3 (*fig. 105*) was furnished with a hypocaust floor heated from the north, a tub with furnace (testudo), a niche for a wash basin (labrum), and a south wall constructed of hollow tiles and revetted with marble. After a destruction in the early 3rd century, the bath was roughly repaired but once again functional. Because of its spatial separation from residential unit 1, the area could have possibly even been rented out and thus used by external individuals.

A particular technical challenge was the constant fire hazard of the praefurnia in the houses. They were usually placed in household areas (e.g. SR 4 and 27) but had to be additionally screened off. A very clever heating system can be found in room 8c of residential unit 4, in which a fire-resistant chimney is hidden behind the apsidal hall where the hot air could escape and be distributed through hollow wall tiles and pipes in the ceiling.

The importance of high hygienic standards and the value of personal hygiene can also be observed in the fact that the water installations were the first things that were repaired and continued to be used after the large earthquake catastrophe in AD 270/280.

Kitchens and Industrial Areas

The kitchens and industrial areas were situated close to the entrance areas. In the archaeological record, they are characterized by simple furnishings and water installations but do not have any other characteristic components. A unique aspect of Terrace House 2 is that industrial areas there were accessible from multiple residential units. Kitchens, latrines, and work areas, as well as small gardens or at least various potted plants could be used by multiple families at the same time. Incised inscriptions in Terrace House 2 also mention animals, which were most likely held in the courtyards of the industrial areas.

Fig. 107: Roman cooking and serving dishes

Most of the kitchens can only be indirectly inferred from cooking and storage vessels (*fig. 107*) and slaughtering waste. The finds from the rooms SR 5a and SR 5c of residential unit 1 are particularly suggestive of kitchen activity: masses of animal bones and charcoaled plant remains were discovered beside a set of cooking dishes as well as a treadwheel of basalt for the production of flour. Grain was only ground when needed –e.g., for making bread– because grain has a substantially longer shelf-life than flour. Since cooking appliances were not found in these rooms, it is likely this equipment was made of metal or clay.

Fig. 108: The kitchen (SR 27a) in residential unit 2

Kitchen installations have only been preserved in the upper story of residential unit 4 as well as in residential unit 2 (*fig. 108*). In residential unit 2, the kitchen (SR 27a) was only installed in the last building phase, around AD 260, and was entered from the peristyle courtyard (SR 22/23). A brick oven was constructed in front of the west wall of the room, above two vaults, and water installations completed the furnishings. The cooking ware and amphorae discovered here are also reliable indicators of the function of the room. In the upper floor of residential unit 4, a baking oven was built into the kitchen (SR 9d) in the 3rd century and probably was used for the production of bread, although it could have also been used as a stove when it was covered. The Roman art of cooking included frying but mainly cooking over the open fire. High-quality pots had to be fire resistant and heat conducting. Made of specific raw materials in specialized pottery shops, they were often traded over thousands of kilometers.

Although these kitchens and the cooking ware support the theory that meals were prepared in Terrace House 2, we cannot underestimate the importance of prepared meals that were offered in taverns and food shops and then brought back to the private home. This very common custom is verified by numerous graffiti mentioning this 'fast food' in the accounts.

Marble Revetment

Slabs of marble and colored stones of approximately 2-3 cm thickness were very popular in Terrace House 2 for the decorative revetment of walls and floors. The conscious use of various types of marble and smoothly pol-

Most of the kitchens can only be indirectly inferred from cooking and storage vessels.

Fig. 109: A figural opus sectile panel from the marble hall (31) in residential unit 6

In building phase IV, around AD 230, marble revetment became the dominant element of the wall decoration and often covered older paintings.

ished surfaces produced a shiny and luminous polychromy, and there is no mistaking that these designs did not fail in their visual effect. Marble revetment decorated the formal areas of houses, including the courtyards as well as the dining and reception rooms, but was also used in rooms with water facilities – the baths, latrines and fountains. This decorative technique ranged from single colored wall revetments to revetments of multiple parts where socle and main zones were of contrasting colors and structured by inlaid frames, to luxurious décor concepts of high-quality and craftsmanship in production as well as in material selection. A pinnacle of this decorative strategy can be found in the figural décor of the opus sectile panels in the marble hall (31) of residential unit 6 (*fig. 109*).

In building phase IV, around AD 230, marble revetment became the dominant element of the wall decoration and often covered older paintings. In order to mount the heavy slabs in the courtyard (24) of residential unit 5, its paintings with red backgrounds were even hacked with little cuts so that the applied mortar bedding would have a stronger bind (*fig. 110*). The increase of marble revetments can be explained by the adoption of decorative luxury associated with the public sphere into the private one and could also be related to a fashion or changed sense of style in the 3rd century. This development can also be well-understood within Terrace House 2: while residential unit 6 was a 'pioneer', expanded into an urbane city residence in the 2nd century already with marble revetment throughout the entire unit, the other actually private houses of the insula only used marble three gen-

Fig. 110: Multi-phase wall décor in residential unit 5

erations later. However, contrary tendencies can also be seen: the owner of residential unit 1 almost entirely dispensed of marble revetted walls and in the 3rd century had his house anachronistically painted.

The taste for marble is also expressed in its abundant imitation in painting and stucco. In these cases, the structure of the painted wall zones as well as the color choice reflects the models. Particularly high-quality examples can be found in room SR 17 of residential unit 1 and also in room 25 of residential unit 5, where a dark red main zone with a white frame can be seen above a green socle zone (*fig. 111*).

Fig. 111: A polychrome stucco décor in room 25 of residential unit 5

Mosaics

Mosaics are the most common decorative surface of floors in Terrace House 2 and were retained over generations due to their rather unspecific decoration, their quality, and their durability. In contrast, the decoration of the walls reflected more current styles and trends. Reasons for installing a mosaic floor included its aesthetic appeal, durability, water impermeability as well as ease of cleaning. Many preserved mosaic floors date as early as the early- and mid-imperial period but were still used in the later 3rd century.

Black-white mosaics with geometric designs were particularly popular in Terrace House 2. Their installation in hallways and entrance areas complemented the flow of movement while the areas in common rooms were decorated with centrally located, carpet-like emblemata, which could be rectangular or square, with geometric or sometimes also figural decoration, and were usually surrounded by a wide, white edge. This gave the impression of a carpet laid on a white floor. Frequently, the central fields of the emblemata stand out because they are more delicate, made of smaller stones than their surroundings, such as room SR 18 in residential

Particularly high-quality examples can be found in room SR 17 of residential unit 1 and also in room 25 of residential unit 5, where a dark red main zone with a white frame can be seen above a green socle zone.

Fig. 112: Mosaic floor of room SR 18 in residential unit 2

Frequently, the central fields of the emblemata stand out because they are more delicate, made of smaller stones than their surroundings, such as room SR 18 in residential unit 2.

unit 2 (*fig. 112*). These were not prefabricated images that were delivered, already premade, by a workshop, and then rolled out; instead, these were specially installed *in situ*, with the goal of emphasizing the particular decorative area and mimicking the expensive prefabricated images.

The heart of the house, including the peristyle courtyards as well as the dining and reception rooms, was accented with polychrome and even figural mosaic floors. This can be observed in residential units 2 and 7, where the hallway floors of the courtyards (SR 22/23 and 38b) were covered with polychrome, geometric pavements in the 2nd and 3rd centuries (*fig. 113*). Also during this time, a figural, painted wall panel was installed in the southern walkway of the peristyle courtyard (SR 22/23), directly linking the floor to the surrounding architecture. On an elongated rectangular field, a nereid rides a hippocamp while a triton is holding his reins and a trident.

Marble slab floors, which were preferable placed in the formal public areas of Terrace House 2, also enhanced the living space. These floors not only decorate the marble hall (31) and the apsidal hall (8) of residential unit 6, but also the peristyle courtyard of residential unit 7 to the south of the adjoining exedra (38), thus contrasting with the colorful mosaics in the porticoes.

The design of the floor mosaics was sometimes directly connected to function of the room. This is the case in dining rooms that have mosaic areas in a U- or TU-form and therefore suggest the presence of klinai or dining couches. The edges of the room concealed by the klinai differ from the service zones in their less elabo-

Fig. 113: Mosaic floor in the walkway of the peristyle courtyard (38b) of residential unit 7

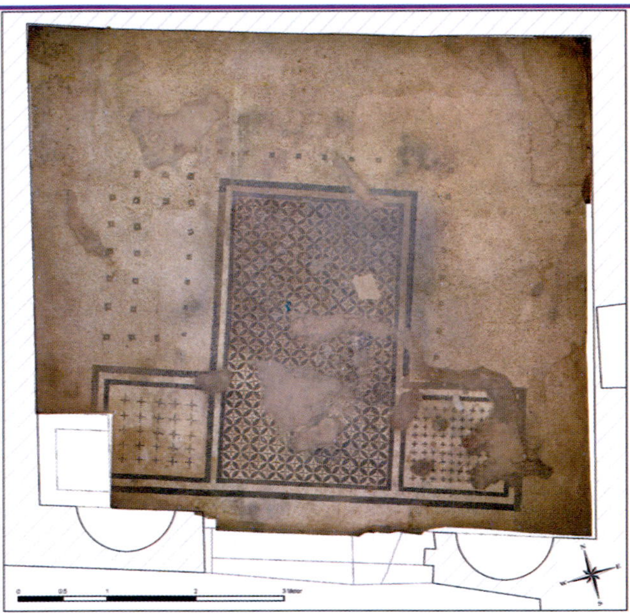

Fig. 114: Mosaic floor in triclinium (SR 24) of residential unit 2

rate and rougher workmanship and simple décor or lack thereof. The best example of this in Terrace House 2 is the triclinium (SR 24) of residential unit 2, where there was enough space for a total of five dining couches (*fig. 114*). However, in the marble hall (31) of residential unit 6, the mosaic strip decorated the space under the klinai while the service area was decorated with marble slabs.

The abundance of mosaics in residential unit 3 is surprising, especially in view of its small size and number of rooms. In this house, four rooms had figural images of which three are still preserved. The mosaic in room 17 from the mid-2nd century AD can be read as a depiction of an amphitheater scene and shows a lion with the bloody, decapitated head of a bull be-

The abundance of mosaics in residential unit 3 is surprising, especially in view of its small size and number of rooms.

tween his paws (*fig. 211*). The small room 16a is located to the south of the peristyle courtyard (16b) and was also decorated with mosaics. The prefabricated images in the middle display the portrait of the god Dionysus wearing an ivy wreath, holding his attribute, the thyrsus staff, in his right hand and the head of Medusa in front of her aegis (*fig. 115*). The use of green and blue gold tesserae for the ivy leaves are particularly

Fig. 115: God Dionysus as central emblem of a mosaic floor

eye-catching, as are the glass cubes with inlaid gold foil for the diadem of the god.

Glass mosaics, extremely expensive and elaborate, were also used for the emphasis of architecturally decorative areas, such as vaults and niches. They were particularly popular for wall and niche fountains, where their luminosity was enhanced by flowing water. In the vaulted rooms, the flickering oil lamps vivifying the polychrome and frequently figural glass mosaics would have produced charming effects. In Terrace House 2, while glass mosaic decorated numerous fountains, it also embellished other kinds of architecture, including the large apse of the hall (8) of residential unit 6. Only fragments have been preserved from most of these examples, however. The best preserved glass mosaics are located in the exedra (GEW D) of residential unit 2. Here Dionysius and Ariadne appear as life-size busts in a central round medallion (*fig. 116*) embedded in a vineyard scene. The Dionysian theme is again referenced with

Fig. 116: Glass mosaic in the exedra of residential unit 2

They were particularly popular for wall and niche fountains, where their luminosity was enhanced by flowing water.

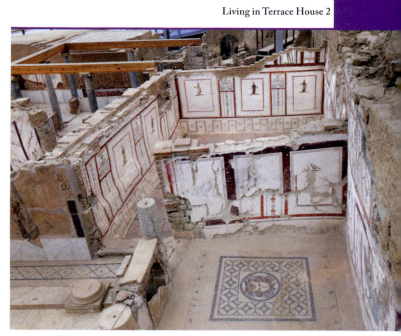

Fig. 117: View onto the room of the muses (12) of residential unit 3

the depiction of two heraldic peacocks in the lunette.

Wall Painting

Over 75 rooms in Terrace House 2 have preserved wall paintings (fig.117); additionally, there are masses of fragments discovered in the rubble that were originally part of the ceilings and upper stories. Paintings were usually adapted to the current trends: only a single painting (room 42 of residential unit 6) remained for two phases of use. As diverse as the wall decoration could be in its designs, its structure always followed a normative system of three horizontal zones.

Above a socle of varying height was a structured main zone, and above this was usu-

Realism blends with fantasy: here it is possible to find chickens or pigeons with the beaks and tails of water fowl.

Fig. 118: Depiction of the philosopher Socrates in residential unit 5

ally a decorated upper zone that was separated from the main zone by a stucco molding or a painted ornamental band. More than half of the paintings in Terrace House 2 follow a structure of lesenes (so-called Felder-Lisenen-Gliederung). This wall system is found in every building phase in a range of qualities, and thus also in rooms of varying significance. Above the socle zone, the central, oblong zones were surrounded by frames and featured emblema, central motifs. The depiction of muses, philosophers (*fig. 118*) or gods, as well as erotes in serving or hunting guises were popular. Animals, such as fish and birds (*fig. 119*), were most frequently de-

Fig. 119: Depiction of a bird on a wall painting

Fig. 120: Scattered flowers painting

picted. Typically, side rooms were decorated with motifs without deeper meaning. Realism blends with fantasy: here it is possible to find chickens or pigeons with the beaks and tails of water fowl. The pictorial fields in these rooms are separated by variously designed lesenes. A frieze of stucco or a painted ornamental zone sets off the main decoration from the upper zone, where usually more architectural paintings were located.

A second decorative wall system that was particularly popular in the 3rd century consisted of scattered flowers (*fig. 120*) that could be further embellished with blossoms, garlands, baskets, birds, and also figural décor. A further characteristic of this system is its multimedia aesthetic, particularly found in the 3rd century taste for marble revetments and their imitation in marble (*fig. 121*).

Changes in living habits and ownership, but also external factors such as destructions, caused quick, responsive redesign. The older wall paintings were carefully chipped away

Fig. 121: Painted imitation of marble slabs

The color choices, ornamental systems, and surface treatment were all determined by the context of the room and the wishes of the patron to create a distinctive and pleasant atmosphere.

and replaced by a new coat of plaster; there are seldom more than three coats on a given wall. While only a few fragments of wall painting have been preserved from building phase I (AD 25-50), complete design ensembles of areas of Terrace House 2 can be reconstructed for the Hadrianic period (building phase II, around AD 120).

In residential unit 4, the main painting zone of the walkway of the courtyard (21) is decorated with lesene-paintings on a dark background. Artistically elaborate and finely worked figural emblemata were set inside red fields structured by frames bordered finely. Only the depictions of the muse Urania (*fig. 122*) and the philosopher Socrates have been preserved, but a cycle of nine muses and seven sages of Greece can be reconstructed. The upper zone is dominated by large mythological scenes, of which the discovery of Achilles on Scyros is still visible *in situ*. It is likely that this is another cycle of images, this time from the Trojan cycle. The wall paintings interacted with the architecture and were also important to the func-

Fig. 122: The muse Urania

tion of the room because they enhanced and emphasized staged visual axes (*fig. 123*). The color choices, ornamental systems, and surface treatment were all determined by the context of the room and the wishes of the patron to create a distinctive and pleasant atmosphere. This applies in particular to the content of the images, which was supposed to convey certain ideas and make bold statements.

The imagery of Terrace House 2 is diverse, including depictions of myths, philosophers, muses, gods, cult images, and also private portraits, erotic scenes, hunt and animal images, garden and landscape paintings, and

Fig. 123: A reconstruction of the courtyard (21) of residential unit 4

even depictions of servants, banquets and daily life. Virtual servants presented the individual entering the room with floors, garlands, and drinks, and served those invited with wine and fish. This was likely both an ideal image of the patron's hospitality and at the same time a reflection of reality. Wall paintings became a method of self-glorification and thus mirrored the environment of the client and his or her social and cultural identity. In this context, the paintings in the courtyard (21) of residential unit 4 can be interpreted easily: while philosophers and muses spoke to the education of the patron, images from Greek mythology –such as the depiction of Achilles who is discovered, dressed as a woman, and summoned to Troy– alluded to the patron's own fulfillment of responsibilities and virtues.

While the patron could count on the widespread knowledge of myths to send such messages to his or her audience, the model of

While the patron could count on the widespread knowledge of myths to send such messages to his or her audience, the model of Classical education could also be ridiculed.

Classical education could also be ridiculed. The caricatures of philosophers and the cartoon of their pseudo-wisdom in the latrine (SR 29) of residential unit 2 clearly illustrate this point (*fig. 124*): the scrawny men are not discussing high truths, but instead the right time, and are thus reminding the users of the latrine to hurry.

Observance of religion and cult can be seen in the courtyard (38b) of residential unit 7, where, in building phase II (around AD 120), a selection of gods are presented in fields of red background; the healing deity Asclepius and the victory goddess Victoria are still preserved (*fig. 125*). This wall painting, as well as painted scenes of offerings in adjoining formal rooms, frame an ensemble of furni-

Fig. 124: Caricature of a philosopher in the latrine (SR 29) of residential unit 2

ture in the center of the courtyard, where an ornate marble table and a round altar with an eagle relief formed an axial view with busts of the emperor Tiberius and his mother Livia in the niche of the southern reception room. Finally, direct connections can be inferred between the paintings and the function of objects that they decorate: for example, the painted fish on a freshwater basin in room 36a of residential unit 6 is evidence of its function as a fish tank – either for edible or ornamental fish.

In Terrace House 2 we can distinguish a clear hierarchy of the wall decoration, one directly connected to room function. Main rooms, such as courtyards and reception and dining rooms, are furnished with figural paintings on a dark background with marble revetment or painted imitations of marble. On the other hand, all other rooms have paintings on a white background of varying quality. While the so-called room of the muses was painted with great love of detail and care, its siderooms and industrial areas were designed with simple bird or fish motifs. Indirectly lit smaller rooms (cellae) were covered with simple, scattered flower motifs.

Fig. 125: Goddess Victoria on the wall painting from the peristyle courtyard (38b) of residential unit 7

An especially thorough redesign took

In Terrace House 2 we can distinguish a clear hierarchy of the wall decoration, one directly connected to room function.

place in building phase IV (around AD 230), which was also a good opportunity for home-owners to bring their wall decorations up-to-date. According to the taste of the time, the main rooms were mainly decorated with marble revetments or its imitation. Less important rooms received paintings of varying quality in lesene-system and scattered flowers. Such a design scheme can be particularly observed in residential unit 2. Here the walls of the peristyle courtyard (SR 22/23) were decorated with marble slab revetment, and above it an upper zone was embellished with an erotes-garland frieze on a blue background (*fig. 126*).

Fig. 126: The erotes-garland frieze in the peristyle courtyard (SR22/23) of residential unit 2

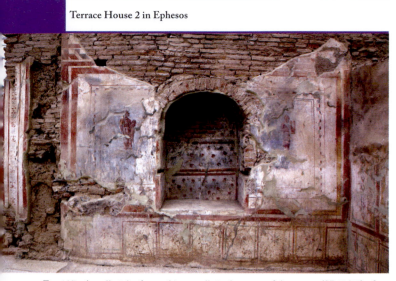

Fig. 127: A wall niche for stacking scrolls in the room of the muses (SR19/20) of residential unit 2

> *Bedrooms of secondary function (SR 25 and 26) are decorated with bird paintings and in the industrial areas.*

The floating erotes are carrying rich garlands filled with fruits that are crossed by fine yellow garlands hanging from peltae-shaped oscilla. The northern reception and dining rooms are also revetted with marble slabs; in the east, an additional reception room (SR 17) engages with the marble revetment and imitates it in elaborately painted stucco. The room of the muses (SR 19/20) is carefully furnished with a lesene system and scattered flowers in the wall cupboards (*fig. 127*). Bedrooms of secondary function (SR 25 and 26) are decorated with bird paintings and in the industrial areas, fish emblemata can be found in the main zone.

The low number of figural images and the ostentatious marble decoration is quite striking.

The wall paintings demonstrate clear differences that are not tied to any style but instead have to do with the depicted genre or the function of the room. This can be impressively demonstrated for the north wall of the so-called theater room (SR 6) of residential unit 1, where different depiction methods were chosen for different contents (*fig. 128*). Theater scenes, painted servants, and the mythological scene in the upper zone were created at the same time, although at first glance they differ stylistically. In addition, the perceived difference in quality between the main and side rooms is noticeable, and it is possible that the frame and filler ornaments were drawn by an apprentice while the central emblemata were designed by the master.

Fig. 128: North wall of the theater room (SR 6) in residential unit 1

Fig. 129: Eros carrying a garland from residential unit 2

Fig. 130: Eros carrying a garland from residential unit 6

The lesene system as well as the scattered flowers are typical of the very traditional and stylistically independent painting craftsmanship of Ephesos. This local style became especially apparent in building phase IV (around AD 230), when one workshop worked in almost all of the residential units of Terrace House 2. Explicit references to the workshop can be found in the peristyle courtyard (SR 22/23) of residential unit 2 and in the vaulted room (36a) of residential unit 6 (*fig. 129. 130*), where the erotes-garland friezes, including the fruit garlands and peltae, correspond even in minute details (*fig. 131. 132*). The background has been designed differently, but this can be explained by the structure of the room: while

36a is a dim, vaulted room, the frieze in the courtyard suggests an illusionary vista into the open and thus complements the open design of the space.

Western, Roman influences can only be detected in rare cases. In residential unit 6, the phase II painting in room 42 very closely corresponds to paintings in Ostia Antica, the harbor city of Rome (*fig. 133*). The Ostian décor is also a lesene system, but it is arranged completely differently: a main zone rises up above a low socle with unusual lesenes and small panels depicting seascapes as emblema (*fig. 134*). The lesene system is repeated in

Fig. 131: A pelta from residential unit 6

The lesene system as well as the scattered flowers are typical of the very traditional and stylistically independent painting craftsmanship of Ephesos.

Fig. 132: A pelta from residential unit 2

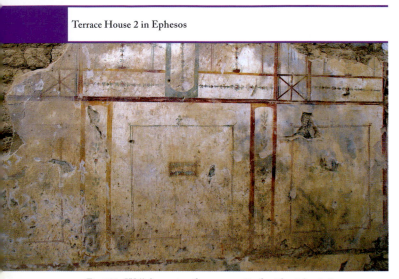

Fig. 133: Wall decoration from room 42 of residential unit 6

the upper zone, but is structured by aediculae filled with birds sitting on blossoming brances. The execution of the painting resembles that of local craftsman who adapted western designs from templates in pattern books. It is likely that this painting was an explicit wish of a particular client, since the architecture and furnishings of residential unit 6 are marked by multifaceted and intense connections to Rome.

Fig. 134: Panel painting with oceanscape from room 42

The lack of real gardens was here compensated by the depiction of a painted landscape with birds and fruit trees, as well as a real water basin, centrally located in the courtyard, which brought nature into the house.

Fig. 135: Garden painting from the courtyard (21) of residential unit 4

Two additional examples illustrate to what extent the design concepts reflected the individual taste of the client. In residential unit 4, the pillar courtyard (21) was decorated with illusionistic garden paintings (*fig. 135*) around AD 150 (building phase III) – this is, to date, the only example of this form of design in Ephesos. The lack of real gardens was here compensated by the depiction of a painted landscape with birds and fruit trees, as well as a real water basin, centrally located in the courtyard, which brought nature into the house. The patron of residential unit 1, on the other hand, completely resisted the general 3rd-century trend by foregoing the stylish marble revetment and instead kept the older, painted wall decoration (*fig. 136*). Figural and

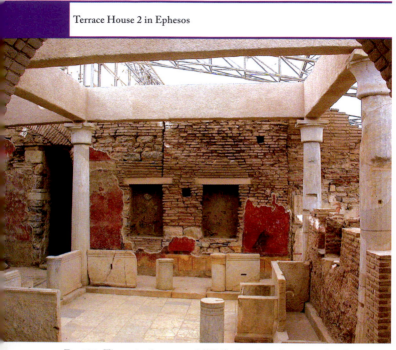

Fig. 136: The peristyle courtyard (SR 2) of residential unit 1 with red as background of painting

mythological depictions –an anachronism in the Severan design concepts of Terrace House 2– were consciously emphasized in this house, and thus the traditionalism of the patron was elevated to a programmatic statement.

Sculpture

The rich sculptural décor in Terrace House 2 includes reliefs and sculptures in-the-round of under-life sized or small-format figures. It is concentrated in the core areas of the individual residential units, the courtyards and reception rooms, and was placed on furniture, walls and ledges, in front of columns, in cupboards, and most frequently in niches in the wall. This idea is supported by the unfinished or rough backs of the sculpted images, making it un-

The original setting of most of the pieces cannot be securely reconstructed because the mostly small sculptures could be easily transported.

Fig. 137: Statuette of the goddess Artemis of residential unit 4

likely that they were set up to be viewed from all sides. White marble, other colored stones, ivory and bronze were the preferred materials. The original setting of most of the pieces cannot be securely reconstructed because the mostly small sculptures could be easily transported.

In this context, the eventful history of the 1.15 m tall Artemis statuette of the Louvre-Ephesos type must be mentioned. The statue was discovered in room 7 of residential unit 4 (*fig. 137*). She was lying in the debris in front of the niche of the west wall, where she was set up in the 3rd century AD on a base with plinth. Before that, however, she decorated the fountain basin in the courtyard (21) for about a century (approximately AD 120-230). The basin was constructed in the early Hadrianic period and was dismantled in the Severan period, filled with debris, and covered with a marble floor, while the Artemis is much older and dates to the late 2nd or early 1st century BC. The statue is an excellent example of a prestigious object that was moved around but probably remained in the house over centuries due to its value as an antique. The 35 cm tall statuette of an Egyptian priest of bronze (*fig. 138*), discovered in residential unit 2, shares a similar story. It can be dated to 610-595 BC based on the inscription on the sash of the priest's coat. 880 years passed between its creation date and last home in Terrace House 2, when the statuette traveled about 1,500 km from Thebes in Upper Egypt to Ephesos.

Fig. 138: Bronze statuette of an Egyptian priest from residential unit 2

It can be dated to 610-595 BC based on the inscription on the sash of the priest's coat.

The architecture, furnishings, and sculpture of a residential unit were sometimes coordinated, but this was not always the case. Since the sculptural décor of a private house was usually not created all at the same time but instead was collected over time, sculpture of varying age, subject, style and also size was exhibited together. The decorative effect of the sculpture

Fig. 139: Burial relief from room 24 of residential unit 5

played an important role –related to the representation of the patron– that also influenced the choice of topic and object.

Miniature herms and genre art depicting everyday scenes were part of the standard furnishings of the house. Reliefs were highly prized art objects (*fig. 139*), and owners did not shy away from showing burial reliefs within the living space of the residential unit. Many sculptures were ambiguous in their function or could assume a range of functions depending on their surroundings. This is the case for images of gods, which could be displayed for cultic-religious or also decorative reasons.

Aphrodite statuettes of terracotta (*fig. 140*) were found in great quantities in Terrace House 2; these mass-produced statuettes were purely decorative objects that can be considered pleasing accessories of table decoration. Sculptures of healing gods such as Isis, Serapis, Asclepius and Hygieia, particularly popular in the 3rd century, must be interpreted differently (*fig. 141*): those venerating the statues hoped for recovery, safety and comfort. Dionysus, the god of wine, enjoyment, and fertility was omnipresent (*fig. 142*). He and his entourage are present on mosaics, wall paintings, stuccos, statues, busts, inscriptions

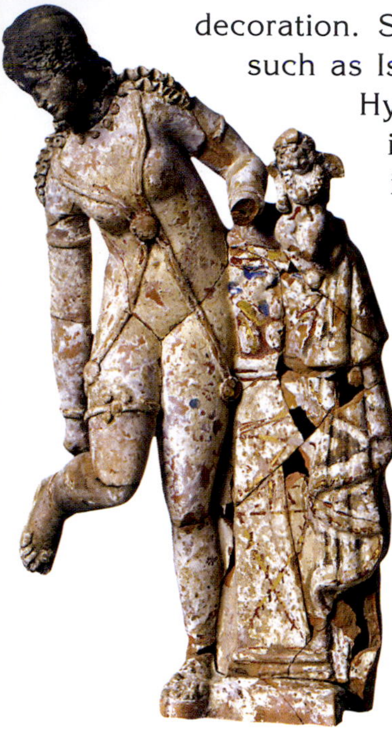

Fig. 140: Terracotta statuette of the goddess Aphrodite opening her sandals from Terrace House 1

and small altars with burning incense. The god appears particularly frequently in residential unit 6, where the owner Gaius Flavius Furius Aptus, as the priest of Dionysius, was in charge of the organization of festivals in honor of the god, the so-called Dionysia.

Fig. 141: Statuette of the goddess Isis-Panthea from residential unit 2

Dionysus, the god of wine, enjoyment, and fertility was omnipresent.

Fig. 142: Head of the god Dionysus

The placement of imperial portraits in private houses can be understood as a sign of loyalty and recognition of the imperial household. Since the boundaries of the private imperial cult are blurry, the careful examination of the original placement of the portraits is needed. This is not possible for a life-sized bust of the emperor Marcus Aurelius (AD 161-180) from residential unit 6 (*fig. 143*): the bust was removed from its original location during ancient renovation work and was temporarily stored in another location. However, the effective presentation of an assortment of statues in one of the peristyle courtyards or large halls of the house can be assumed. The patron might have been motivated by a personal

Fig. 143: Bust of the emperor Marcus Aurelius

Fig. 144: Private portrait of a bearded man

bond and thankfulness towards the imperial house in general, or the Antonine dynasty in particular.

Numerous, usually small-format private portraits are likely to have been images of members of the owner's family that were put on display in prominent places. They reflect the need for self-display and class-consciousness, which was further enhanced by the artistic quality of the sculptures and the choice of expensive materials.

Two small-format busts were originally set up in the northern reception rooms of residential unit 2. The head of a 20 cm tall, male portrait from the triclinium (SR 24) is made of marble and the bust of alabaster (calcite) (*fig. 144*). The short hair, the eyes with incised iris and drilling of the pupil, the deeply furrowed brow as well as the molded beard are typical features of portraits from the first half of the 3rd century AD, and thus date the placement to the last phase of use of the house. This dating also applies to a portrait of a boy of equal size from the room (SR 28) adjoining in the west. It is made entirely of pavonazzeto marble (*fig. 145*). The boy is dressed in a tunic and a fringed cloak,

Fig. 145: Private portrait of a boy

Fig. 146: Family portraits made of ivory

held together at his right shoulder by a disk brooch. In the same room were found three small-format, charcoaled ivory portraits of late-Severan date (around AD 220/230); their composition of man, woman, and child were likely a family ensemble (*fig. 146*). A statuette of a seated togatus from room SR 18 (*fig. 147*), originally about 30 cm tall, is made of a variety of colored stones and reflects senatorial class-consciousness. Al-

The boy is dressed in a tunic and a fringed cloak, held together at his right shoulder by a disk brooch.

Fig. 147: Seated statuette from residential unit 2

Graffiti, or engraved inscriptions, are found in great quantity on the walls of Terrace House 2.

though his head is sadly not preserved, the toga worn over a tunic, the right arm raised in oration gesture, the rank-specific shoes (calceus senatorius), and the throne, the sella curulis, indicate that the individual depicted was a member of the senatorial class, or possibly even the emperor. This sculpture, from the first half of the 2nd century AD, survived multiple family generations and their fates, until it was damaged by a large earthquake around AD 270/280 and then buried.

Graffiti and Dipinti

Graffiti, or engraved inscriptions, are found in great quantity on the walls of Terrace House 2. They are an extremely interesting body of evidence because they are direct proof for the actual use of rooms. Their authors, standing in front of the very same walls as the modern visitor of the Terrace House and inscribed texts or drawings onto the wall reflecting a certain life situation. Inhibitions from etching into the walls appear to have been fairly low because the quantity of graffiti is surprisingly high. At times, the content or location of the inscription might have been less pleasing, but sometimes even high-ranking family members placed texts in easily visible places in order to enhance their status with their comment. The graffiti were usually written in Greek; Latin graffiti exist in larger quantities in residential unit 6.

The engraved inscriptions are spread across multiple rooms but are especially numerous in the courtyards and latrines, presenting an important source for daily culture as they commemorate certain events. Epigrams, birth announcements, commemorations, word and number puzzles, and thank you notes to the hosts are found on the walls. The many graffiti expressing gratitude of guests and praise of the hosts in the main rooms give the impression that the walls were used as a form of a guest book after a meal. On the garden painting in the courtyard (21) of residential unit 4, the following thank you note is recorded: "Attalianos, the boy, commemorated the beautiful hospitality!". Thank you notes are preserved even on painting fragments from the upper story of residential unit 4, verifying the staging of dinners even in the upper stories.

Inscribed blessings are also found throughout the Terrace House, and frequently one blessing encouraged many more – as, for example, on a single pillar on the north wall of the courtyard (21) of residential unit 4: "May you have good luck!"; "May you have bad luck!"; "Be happy Eutychios, in many years!"; and finally, "May you live, Akakios, be happy, beautiful boy!"

Alphabets and lines of numbers could have been written by children as writing practice, because they have been found at a low height. And, as still common today, the walls were

Toilet humor graffiti

used by happy or unhappy lovers for messages filled with emotion.

Graffiti of suggestive or even vulgar content are not uncommon, as are messages referring to hetero- or homosexual tendencies and practices. Particularly in latrines, crude language is commonplace.

Lists of expenditures are particularly interesting, as they probably are accounts of entrusted funds (*fig. 148. 149*). They consist of two columns: on the left side, purchases and services are noted, while expenditures are noted on the right. The lists are in units of denarii, sesterces, and assaria, copper money that circulated in the east of the Roman Empire and was minted until the reign of the emperor Gallienus (AD 253-268). Various foods,

Fig. 148: Expenditure lists etched into the walls

ΚΑΡΗ ΔΙC	(Hasel-?) nut 10 ¹/₂ asses
CΥΚΥΔΙΔ	Small figs 2 ¹/₂ asses
ΚΡΕΙΘΛΙ	Barley 12 denarii ¹/₂ ass
ΚΑΛΙΤΥΧΗ	For Kallityche 1 denarius
ΞΥΛΔ	Wood 3 asses
ΚΡΟΗΟΙΔ	Onions 3 asses
ΓΑΥΔ	Caraway ¹/₂ ass
ΕΙΒΑΛΔΝΗ	(Entrance) to the thermal bath 12 asses

Fig. 149: Drawing and translation of an expenditure list

Lists of expenditures are particularly interesting, as they probably are accounts of entrusted funds.

Fig. 150: A wall inscription with the depiction of the goddess Athena

firewood, cleaning detergents as well as craftsmen services for plumbing work or for laying a mosaic floor are enumerated. Even the cost of entrance to the public baths and the price of prostitutes were recorded on the walls.

The walls, besides from being easy writing surfaces, were also used as drawing surfaces. The spectrum ranges from simple geometric motifs to ship depictions, animals and hunting scenes, to depictions of humans and gods. A pretty profile of Athena Parthenos (*fig. 150*) particularly stands out. A wish from residential unit 4, addressing Roma and the stability of the entire political system, fits into this context: "Rome, you dominator of the universe, may your power never fade!".

Depictions of gladiators (*fig. 151*) were particularly popular and frequent. They were celebrated as heroes and probably had many fans in Terrace House 2.

Fig. 151: A wall inscription with the depiction of gladiators

Fig. 152: Painted theater scenes with inscriptions

Regarding spices, herbs, garum (a salty fish sauce), vinegar and caraway seed are mentioned; honey was used as a preservative and sweeting agent.

Dipinti, or painted inscriptions, usually give additional information about characters or scenes depicted in wall decoration (*fig. 152*). In the peristyle courtyard (24) of residential unit 5, examples of this can be found in the names above the muses and also the round medallions with philosopher portraits. The titles of the depicted tragedies and comedies are also found above the theater scenes in the theater room (SR 6) of residential unit 1. A special dipinto is legible on the back of a marble revetment panel in the marble hall (31) of residential unit 6. Here the Latin inscription *Furi Apti* ("for Furius Aptus") mentions the delivery address for the marble block.

Diet and Food

While the ordinary people mainly lived off of flatbread and bread as well as porridge based on grains or legumes, the menu of the upper class –whom we encounter in Terrace House 2– was completely different and diverse. The

main meal, the cena, was consumed in the later afternoon
and often lasted for a couple of
hours. The variation in the dining culture of the inhabitants
of the Terrace House is illustrated by different kinds of evidence, including the account-
ing lists that were etched onto
the house walls, animal bones,
charcoaled plant remains, as
well as transport and storage
dishes that were found onsite.
In this way we get a general
sense of the purchased fruit
and vegetables, including arti-
chokes, beans, lentils, onions,

Fig. 153: Clay mould for the production of breads

figs, cucurbita (probably cantaloupe), grapes,
and hazelnuts. Regarding spices, herbs, garum
(a salty fish sauce), vinegar and caraway seed
are mentioned; honey was used as a preservative and sweeting agent. There were deliveries
of bread and ready-made meals. Of course,
bread and flatbread were also made in the
house, as the purchase of barley and millet
suggests. For particularly elaborate breads or
cakes, figural clay models were used, such as
the ones found in residential unit 1 that depict
a group of animals including a rabbit, elephant,
and vulture (fig. 153). Bread in pyramid shape
was also decoratively placed on the banquet
tables. Olive oil was the basis of vegetable and
meat dishes and was therefore frequently re-
quested and billed. Olive seeds have been discovered, which must have come from the fruits

Fig. 154: An imported wine amphora from Crete

The lesser importance of the hunt is reflected by the small percentage of game in the bone remains.

themselves, commonly served as a side dish.

Drinks are often mentioned in the graffiti, including grape juice, but surprisingly, also water. This might be referring to the popular ice water that was used for cooling wine. Oil extracted from the jojoba fruit was also used to make a bitter tasting juice. The majority of the graffiti refer to specific types of wine, from Samos or Italy, for example, but also to wine that was delivered to Terrace House 2 already flavored with thyme. The many varieties of wine consumed in Terrace House 2 can also be demonstrated based on amphorae discovered by excavators (*fig. 154*). Although the basic needs of the residents of Terrace House 2 were covered by regional products produced in the hinterland of Ephesos, their sophisticated dining culture required that special varietals and vintages were served. It is understandable that wines from different Aegean islands, the Greek mainland, the Black Sea, as well as Italy and the Levant were found on the tables of Ephesian dignitaries.

While the sausages mentioned in the graffiti were probably ordered, preparation of meat dishes clearly took place on site. This is indicated by traces of hacking on animal bones and the evidence of dissected remains, typical of kitchen waste. Pig was especially popular and was butchered at the best age; the meat of sheep/goats, and cows was also consumed. Other preferred meat included poultry, especially chickens, as well as ducks, geese, peacocks, pheasants, doves, great bustards, and rock partridge. Chickens were butchered when they were full grown and apparently all parts were used as indicated by the discovery of foot bones. The eggs of domesticated and wild fowl were often prepared, preferably for breakfast (lentaculum) or lunch (prandium). The dinners in Terrace House 2 were distinguished by the exclusivity of the dishes served; these included deliciously prepared song birds such as quails, larks, thrushes, finches, and swallows. The lesser importance of the hunt is reflected by the small percentage of game in the bone

Fig. 155: Residential unit 3, room 16a: wrasse

Fig. 156: *Symphodus tinca*: peacock wrasse

remains. With the exception of wild fowl and rabbits, which were prepared more frequently, wild boar, red deer, and fallow deer seem to have been foreign to the tables of the inhabitants of the Terrace House.

Fish and seafood (*fig. 155. 156*) provided an adequate supply of proteins and were consumed in large quantities. Alongside typical ocean fish such as gilt-head bream, mackerel, mullet, tuna and shark, wrasse and flatfish came from coastal fisheries. The very popular and frequently consumed fresh water fish, such as carp, zander, common bream, and roach, were caught in lakes, ponds and rivers in the hinterland of Ephesos or even farmed in basins. The fishing business was an extremely successful line of business –either on the open seas, along the coasts, in the lakes in the hinterland or through cultivation– and probably did not only serve the immediate region. As the preserved fish tanks indicate, fish were also held in the houses –at least for short periods– and prepared fresh. It is possible that important guests were even allowed to choose their own fish.

Clams were a favorite, above all the cockle (*fig. 157*). The

Fig. 157: Edible mussels from residential unit 1

The amount of large, edible land snails is also high while other types of snails and mollusks did not play a big role.

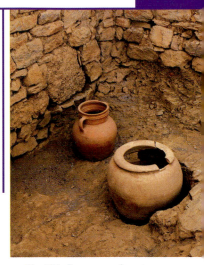

Fig. 158: Storage vessels set into the ground

amount of large, edible land snails is also high while other types of snails and mollusks did not play a big role. The most important clams, such as the cockle, the zebra mussel, or the Japanese carpet shell, were dug out of the sand along the coast in shallow waters, while mussels were found in shallow waters attached to rocks, from which they had to be removed. Diving for scallops in deep waters required greater effort. Oysters, murexes, and land snails were possibly also cultivated.

The food products were transported, stored and preserved in large vessels –pithoi, for example (*fig. 158*)– that were sunk into the ground. It is only rarely possible to identify the content of the jars. An exception is a small jar with

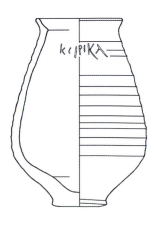

Fig. 159: A jug with the inscription "honey"

Fig. 160: Mortar of marble

the inscription for "honey" on the outside (*fig. 159*). Utensils for the preparation of meals have also been found. These include dial balances as well as basins, bowls, saucepans, lids, and spoons, all made of bronze. Grains and spices were crushed with a mortar (*fig. 160*) or mortarium and pestle, both made of marble. Clay mortaria, completely lacking in Asia Minor, are considered a sign of romanization in other areas. As a result, an imported mortarium from Syria, found in Terrace House 2, seems out of place and almost foreign, possibly an indication of foreign cooking customs and the preparation of exotic dishes.

In the elegant households of Terrace House 2, the prepared meals were served on platters and in bowls already carved and cut into mouth-sized pieces. Sauces, small appetizers, pickled vegetables, and fruit were arranged in small bowls that were placed on side tables. Attendants served the reclined guests, since it was considered impolite to get up during the meal, even to visit the latrine. At the table it was common to take the food with the finger tips or with small spoons (*fig. 161*). The pointed end of the spoon could also

Fig. 161: A silver spoon

be used as a skewer and took the place of the fork in antiquity. Drinks were served in jugs and consumed with cups, usually of glass or clay. Water was also readily available in the dining rooms from the water fountains installed there.

Expensive, richly decorated dishes of precious metal and glass were considered the epitome of Roman dining luxury, but they are only seldom preserved today. The original composition of the set of dishes in Terrace House 2 can therefore not be reconstructed, and we must refer to dishes of other materials in order to gain an impression of the quality and variety of what once was. Along these lines, a fine piece of evidence was discovered in residential unit 2. It is of a form that imitates metal that was particularly popular in the 3rd century AD (*fig. 162*), and its dark-blue glass must have

Fig. 162: A blue glass plate for serving food

Water was also readily available in the dining rooms from the water fountains installed there.

greatly contrasted with other dishes assembled on the platter. Bronze bowls, pitchers, and jugs were also used as serving dishes.

Jugs of clay were very common in daily life and had a trefoil mouth for ease of pouring. There were countless plates and little bowls of varying forms in terra sigillata, a red shining Roman tableware of fired clay. This was mass-produced in large production centers and was widely traded. Thus, it is not surprising to find in Terrace House 2 terra sigillata dishes from Italy, North Africa, the Black Sea, as well as from manufactures in Asia Minor (*fig. 163*). The dishes predominantly originate from potteries located close to Tralles, in the large Meander valley, which had the task of providing the cities along the western coast of Asia Minor, first and foremost Ephesos, with clay tableware.

Fig. 163: A Roman dinner set

Drinking ware consisted of jugs and cups of glass or clay (*fig. 164*). A small sieve spoon was also necessary to strain the added spices out of the wine. Sometimes the pitchers also had small sieves. Eggshell thin clay cups were especially popular in the early Roman Imperial period and were used for drinking. While metal dishes were at some point melted down and thus

Fig. 164: A Roman drinking beaker

lost, those of organic materials did not withstand the storage conditions in the earth and decomposed long ago. Ancient households must have had a large quantity of jars and items of daily use made of wood or basketwork; we can postulate the same for those in Terrace House 2.

Reception and Hosting of Guests

The function of rich peristyle houses, such as those constructed with different variations in Terrace House 2, was not limited to the purely private life of a Roman familia: the house also served as the public stage of the patron for the demonstration of his social and/or commercial responsibilities. From the salutatio, the morning greeting, performed by his clients, to the evening convivium or symposium with invited guests, the peristyle and reception areas were open to visitors. In turn, their opinions of the patron were influenced by the architecture and decoration. The furnishings not only embellished the visual atmosphere; they also conveyed or affirmed social values and educational ideals. At Terrace House 2, the function of rooms is deduced by their size, location within the house and spatial relationship with other rooms, as well as their furnishings discovered in the room, position of doors

Drinking ware consisted of jugs and cups of glass or clay.

and windows, and thus also their lighting and climate conditions. This is particularly the case for the exposed reception rooms that were used for hosting and dining.

Reception rooms, adjoining the peristyle courtyard, were part of the core area of the house (*fig. 165*). In Terrace House 2, often the room type of an exedra, a niche-like room, was selected for reception; its entire length opened up onto the courtyard and was embellished by column and pilaster placements. Those entering were supposed to be impressed by the elaborate design and central location of these rooms, intersecting the visual axes of domestic space.

In order to comply with the social needs of the house owner, neither cost nor effort was spared, as can be appreciated in the last decorative phase of the exedra (GEW D) of residential unit 2. Here the architecture and dec-

Fig. 165: View of the exedra of residential unit 2

Reception rooms, adjoining the peristyle courtyard, were part of the core area of the house.

oration directly reference each other, as the courtyard and exedra, joined together to form a room ensemble, are in visual communication. The walls of the courtyard have a grey-black marble revetment in the socle zone, and in the central zone a white-grey marble revetment; this effectually contrasts with the white socle and dark-grey main slabs in the exedra. The wall painting of the upper zone features erotes holding fruit garlands on a blue background, while the vaulted ceiling and the lunette of the exedra is decorated with a glass mosaic. Also in the courtyard, an elongated, figural mosaic field contrasts with an opus sectile floor made of various colored marbles in the exedra. The mosaic in the courtyard refers to the exedra through its size, location, as well as the orientation of its figures. Behind it a fountain was installed and the constantly flowing water guaranteed a comfortably cool room climate. This luxurious atmosphere must have impressed individuals entering the house during the city's hot, dusty, and loud summer months.

Rooms for the reception and hosting of guests are numerous and variously designed in Terrace House 2. They are marked by their spaciousness, their prominent location with-

Fig. 166: View from the triclinium (SR 24) onto the exedra of residential unit 2

The nine muses were the main theme of decoration, at times accompanied by Apollo Musagetes, the god of music and song, as well as the lyric poet Sappho.

in the house, as well as their furnishing; frequently, specific installations or furniture suggest that symposia took place in them (*fig. 166*). Multiple couches or klinai, on which guests reclined, fit into these rooms. The success of a dinner was measured by its excellent cooking, the lavish atmosphere, and especially the outstanding entertainment; accordingly, enough free space had to be available for musicians, recitations, and sometimes even dancers.

In room (SR 24) of residential unit 2, there was enough space for a maximum of five klinai; up to 15 people could take part at a dinner here. The mosaic floor reflects the placement of the couches and clearly identifies the room as a triclinium. A platform in the south-west corner and another in the theat-

Fig. 167: Marble table from the triclinium (SR 24)

er room SR 6 (*fig. 168*) in residential unit 1 were probably used for the preparation of dishes or for setting a brazier. The sophisticated decoration of this room included white-grey marble wall revetment and a painted ceiling. Two niche fountains lined with glass mosaic were set into the south wall to the right and left of the wide folding doors. They guaranteed a comfortable room climate and provided drinking water for the symposiasts. A showy marble table (*fig. 167*), where possibly two small-format portrait busts were displayed, and a bronze side table completed the stately interior décor. In addition, it was possible to directly communicate with people in the peristyle courtyard –when the door was open– and also with people in the exedra, aligned on the same visual axis.

The so-called rooms of the muses were also used for reception of guests and are found in residential units 2-5. Due to their central locations close to the court-

Fig. 168: A built platform in the theater room (SR 6) of residential unit 1

Fig. 169: Depiction of the muse Terpsichore in the room of the muses (12) in residential unit 3

yards, these rooms were more important (*fig. 169*). The nine muses were the main theme of decoration, at times accompanied by Apollo Musagetes, the god of music and song, as well as the lyric poet Sappho. Having died around 570 BC, Sappho was considered the tenth muse already in antiquity. In the particularly well preserved room of the muses (12) of residential unit 3, the upper zone was decorated with a theater scene featuring three actors wearing buskins. This scene underscores the musical and artistical connotation of the room type. Two marble bases, on which large decorative vases could be displayed, were sunk into the brick tile floor. The room of the muses (SR 19/20) and the room SR 18 of residential unit 2 had niches in the wall with built-in wood shelves where scrolls were kept (*fig. 170*), and also precious items put on display. While the

Fig. 170: The niche in the wall of room SR 18 of residential unit 2

wall decoration suggests that the so-called room of the muses was used for the entertainment of guests with music, dance and theatrical performances, the wine amphorae discovered in the corners also suggest that guests were hosted in these rooms.

In building phase III (around AD 150), at least the ground floor of residential unit 6 was exclusively used for the reception of guests: utility and private areas are completely lacking. Architecture and furnishings followed a carefully planned and well thought out concept that was completely focused on the hosting of guests as well as the organization of assemblies, dinners, and festivities. The hierarchy of the rooms culminated in the large halls (31 and 8) in the south part of the residential unit, adorned with luxurious furnishings that barely could be surpassed and where audiences were received and banquets held.

Furniture

In ancient houses, two types of furniture and furnishings must be differentiated: fixed and moveable. The fixed kind of furniture had set locations that were taken into consideration during construction. These included the built platforms in the dining rooms where dishes were prepared or where braziers were placed

In ancient houses, two types of furniture and furnishings must be differentiated: fixed and moveable.

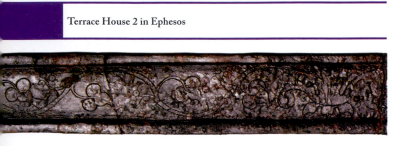

Fig. 171: Inlay of a reclining couch, so-called kline

Residential units 2 and 5 were especially rich in furniture: the majority of the preserved tables, chairs and klinai were found here.

in the cold seasons. But shelves, niches, and cupboards in the walls were also part of this category. On the other hand –and this includes the majority– there was moveable furniture, which was set up depending on its use and the need of its availability. Mobility within the house, flexibility, and multi-functionality of rooms are characteristics of ancient housing culture. Particularly luxurious furniture, apart from its functional use, could be placed out for display. Metal, especially iron and bronze, as well as wood, were common materials, but only the non-perishable fittings and cladding of wooden objects have been preserved.

Residential units 2 and 5 were especially rich in furniture: the majority of the preserved tables, chairs and klinai were found here. Of these ancient couches, only the border rails of the wooden frame have been preserved (*fig. 171*) because the actual wooden elements disintegrated long ago. The front of these rails was artistically decorated with plant motifs in silver damascening, or inlay, and gives a vague impression of the original splendor of the carefully turned and carved klinai in the dining rooms of Terrace House 2.

The tables were between 70 cm and 1 m high (*fig. 172*) and consisted of a frame of three or four feet and a framed board of wood or stone. The folding mechanism and removable board made it possible to collapse the klinai and easily transport them. Tables of this type could be placed by the klinai when needed and were used as a side board or

Fig. 172: Frame of a bronze side table

for the preparation of dishes and drinks. The sculptural décor of the table legs was often very intricate and the feet were frequently designed as the paws of predators. For the three examples found in Terrace House 2, a satyr-boy, a Dionysius bust, and a boxer figure functioned as the bearers of the table top (*fig. 173*). Moreover, a massive table 1.17 m high of rosso brec-

Fig. 173: Detail of a table frame: boxer

Fig. 174: Bronze folding chair

ciato, a Carian, colored marble (*fig. 167*), stood in the triclinium (SR 24) of residential unit 2. The table was design to be seen from the front and consists of three separate parts: an elongated base, the central table leg with cat's paws, the lion protome, and the table top. Due to its height, it was not suited for the preparation of dishes; instead, it was likely one of the reception tables that was used for the display of valuables, luxurious dishes, terracotta groups, or small-format sculpture.

Of the 60 and 43 cm high folding chairs with straight legs, only the frame of iron and bronze remains (*fig. 174*): a seat pad of cloth or preferably leather had been originally attached. On top was a cushion, and a footstool could be added for greater comfort.

In antiquity, objects, clothing, and household goods were stored in chests and boxes.

Fig. 175: Decorative plaques of ivory with depiction of scenes

Because they were mainly made of wood, they can now only be deduced by the preserved metal parts. These include locks, handles, knobs, and sometimes also decorative cladding and reinforcement plates. Inlay of polychrome or glass cut into figures aided the magnificent appearance of these furnishings. This is true in particular for the pieces of furniture that were once decorated with carved ivory plaques discovered in room SR 18 in residential unit 2. In addition to the large Trajanic frieze as well as the reliefs of smaller battle and theater scenes (*fig. 175*), there are multiple individual plaques that were originally attached to chests, boxes, klinai, and doors (*fig. 176*).

We must also mention the furnishings made of marble, generally part of the moveable inventory but too heavy to be moved easily. These include a decorative vessel from the room of the muses (12) of residential unit

Of the 60 and 43 cm high folding chairs with straight legs, only the frame of iron and bronze remains.

Fig. 176: Small decorative plaques of ivory

Fig. 177: Altar and table in residential unit 7

> *Rings with gems were used to mark sealed property and documents and were considered a status symbol for Roman men.*

3, as well as the altar and table ensemble in the peristyle courtyard (38b) of residential unit 7 (*fig. 177*).

Jewelry and Personal Items

Many areas of Terrace House 2 were being renovated when the large earthquake catastrophe hit (AD 270/280); for this reason they were not inhabited, and this explains the relative lack of personal items found by excavators. Needles of bronze and especially of bone, which Roman women used to pin up their hair stylishly and hold it in place, were found in larger quantities. In contrast, fibula are elements of the dress that do not appear frequently in the eastern Roman Empire due to different, brooch-less dress customs.

As has been mentioned, jewelry was only found in surprisingly small quantities. Excavated examples include mostly finger rings, but also glass beads as parts of necklaces, glass bracelets, bronze pendants, and chain links. A massive gold ring with an engraved gem (*fig. 178*) from residential unit 2 dates to the Trajanic period and probably was an heirloom. The engraved image shows a mouse blowing into a double aulos or flute. Rings with gems were used to mark sealed property and documents and were considered a status symbol for Roman men. In SR 26 of residential unit 2, the house owner probably was visiting the freshly finished wall paintings around AD 230 and noticed that the plaster was still soft and malle-

Fig. 178: Ring with a depiction of a mouse playing a flute

Fig. 179: Distaff with a depiction of the goddess Aphrodite

able. Twice he pressed his seal ring into the plaster, and from these one impression is good: the impression of finger bones are clearly recognizable, as well as the fact that he wore the ring on his ring finger. The stone of the ring is engraved with a favorite motif of the 3rd century AD, the goddess of fortune Fortuna, who steers the rudder of fate with one hand and holds a richly filled cornucopia with the other.

While only the hooks remain of wooden spindles, preserved sewing and net needles, loom weights and spinning utensils, distaff and whorl all suggest utilitarian housework. The elaborate distaff discovered in residential unit 2 (*fig. 179*) can be interpreted as a status symbol of the Roman matron. The term 'Venus distaff' describes the upper end of the tool, carved in low relief, and depicts the figure of the half-naked Venus pudica with a dolphin beside her right leg. Elaborate distaffs were favorite wedding presents that were carefully kept and later placed with the deceased in her grave.

Fig. 180: Small bronze bells

The term 'Venus distaff' describes the upper end of the tool, carved in low relief, and depicts the figure of the half-naked Venus pudica with a dolphin beside her right leg.

Fig. 181: A glass oil flask

The function of the simple and variously sized bronze bells (*fig. 180*) of the Roman period can barely be differentiated from their function today. They were used as alarms and could be attached to curtains so that they would chime at the slightest movement, even a slight air current. They were also tied around the necks of animals and even attached to children because the ringing was considered apotropaic and averted evil.

The finds include very few toilette articles for hygiene and cosmetic use. Substances, ground to powder with rubbing stones, were mixed on makeup pallets and then applied to the skin with spatulas. Oils and other essences were kept in ungentaria, small oil bottles. (*fig. 181*). Many of these bottles have been preserved in Terrace House 2 and are made of stone, glass, and mostly pottery. The purchase of ointments, soaps, and cleaning agents is also mentioned in graffiti. Ear picks or scoops served proper hygiene and medical purposes and were kept with other utensils in so-called utensil tins.

Styli, writing pens, game pieces and dice were used for writing and playing.

Large, heavy tools such as axes, heavy hammers, chisels, hoes, and trowels can be associated with the ongoing renovations, while items like the beam balance and bowls were part of the household. The wagon parts discovered in residential unit 2 and 4 might be surprising at first glance. It is probable that the valuable parts of the carriages –as well as the animals– were held in the industrial areas of the houses when not in use.

Objects for the House Cult

Religion and cult were vital elements of daily life in antiquity. Typical cult areas within the household were the hearths and house shrines, where the rituals of the head of the family, the pater familias, took place. A multitude of cults were practiced in the private house. In addition to the veneration of gods and emperors was the ancestral cult, as well as the belief in magic, magical powers, and spirits.

Fig. 182: Building sacrifice from residential unit 4

In celebration of the completion of a house or a renovation, building

Generally, they were simple wall niches with statuettes and incense burners, or just particular wall painting in front of which a moveable altar was set up.

sacrifices were offered (*fig. 182*). Carefully and repeatedly deposited ensembles of dishes were found under the floors in Terrace House 2; in addition, pits with the remains of ritual feasts have been discovered, likely evidence of ritual in the course of construction.

House shrines greatly differed in size, quality and make. Generally, they were simple wall niches with statuettes and incense burners, or just particular wall painting in front of which a moveable altar was set up.

More elaborate variations of the house shrine include aediculae, rooms dedicated solely to the house cult, which were structured by small columns (*fig. 183*). Such a room was discovered in residential unit 4, where there is a wall painting of a red snake straightening up out of its eight coils on a white background (*fig. 184*), as well as two reliefs of funeral feasts. Snakes were supposed to protect the house and its inhabitants in their function of averting evil. The funeral

Fig. 183: The aedicula in room 31b in residential unit 6

Fig. 184: A painted snake in room 5 of residential unit 4

Fig. 185: Relief of hero in residential unit 2

feast reliefs belong to a larger group in the Terrace House associated with the domestic ancestral cult: the reclining deceased is drinking or eating on a kline, surrounded by his or her relatives. A second example of this is in a niche of the peristyle courtyard (SR 22/23) in residential unit 2 (*fig. 185*). The central figure –a young rider– probably represents someone who died too young and was heroized in death. The relief was at least three centuries older than the rest of the interior and was used to remember the deceased ancestors, who also protected the house and family.

Evidence for the cultic veneration of Roman emperors was also found in Terrace House 2. The owner of residential unit 2, Vibius Salutaris, had silver statues of the emperor Trajan and his wife Plotina set up in his private house; before them he practiced rituals on the appropriate days in honor of the imperial couple. It is possible that these rituals took place in the so-called ivory room (SR 18), where a long

Fig. 186: Excerpt of the large ivory frieze: depictions of the emperor Trajan

The owner of residential unit 2, Vibius Salutaris, had silver statues of the emperor Trajan and his wife Plotina set up in his private house.

ivory frieze was discovered that depicts the emperor Trajan with his entourage and also a delegation of barbarians (*fig. 186*).

In the course of the 3rd century AD, healing and mystery gods began taking the place of the traditional Greek gods. The Egyptian cults were very popular, especially those of Sarapis, Isis and Osiris, because of their promise of eternal life and resurrection after death. This development also reached Terrace House 2. In residential unit 2, the statuettes of Isis Panthea, Sarapis, and Athena formed an ensemble with a bronze incense burner that can likely be linked to the house cult. Numerous small clay incense altars were set up in the entrance areas of the houses and were decorated with the bust of Sarapis that identify them as thymiateria with laterally attached lamps (*fig. 187*). In the central incense altar, people could bring offerings to the god, while the lamps provided light. The god Sarapis was omnipresent in Terrace House 2 in the 3rd century, as is demonstrated by the statuettes, busts, and lamps. Syn-

Fig. 187: A Sarapis thymiaterion

Fig. 188: Gem with depiction of the demon Abraxas

The powers of magic, demons, and ghosts were disputed in antiquity.

cretistic   Egyptian belief systems must have been embraced by a large part of the population in the metropolis of Asia Minor in the earlier imperial period.

The powers of magic, demons, and ghosts were disputed in antiquity. Magical gems were set in finger rings or necklace pendants, and also worn on the body sewn into clothing. On an excellent find from Terrace House 2, the Egyptian demon Abraxas is depicted with a rooster's head and snake feet, holding a whip and shield (*fig. 188*). In the 2nd century AD, Abraxas was venerated as a divine power and master of the sun year, of infinity and eternity; by simply pronouncing his name, evil could be brought onto a person, but it could also provide protection.

The residents of Terrace House 2

Terrace House 2 provides a wealth of information about ancient life but it also gives us information about the families who owned and lived in the houses during the Roman imperial period. In the latrine (SR 29) of residential unit 2, not especially flattering graffiti have been preserved that name a certain Salutaris as the owner, asking him to perform both hetero- and homosexual acts. The author was probably addressing Gaius Vibius Salutaris, who was in charge of certain offices in Ephesos in the Trajanic period. As a member of the Roman equestrian order with Italic roots, he was closely associated with the imperial family, in particular the emperor Trajan (AD 98-117). He was also the one who had statuettes of the emperor and his wife Plotina set up in his private house, after they were displayed during the public assembly in the Great Theater of Ephesos and venerated there. Of course, it is not certain whether residential unit 2 was still owned by the same family in the 3rd century AD, but the presence of the so-called ivory room with artwork of the Trajanic period, such as the togatus or the ivory frieze, do support this theory. Although the numerous private portraits of the 3rd century discovered in residential unit 2 are not inscribed with names, they do illustrate the high social rank and self-esteem of the owners. A 36 cm tall standard of bronze can also be understood as a status symbol. It was discovered in the entrance courtyard (SR 27) and was the top of the lance of a beneficiarius (*fig. 189*). Bene-

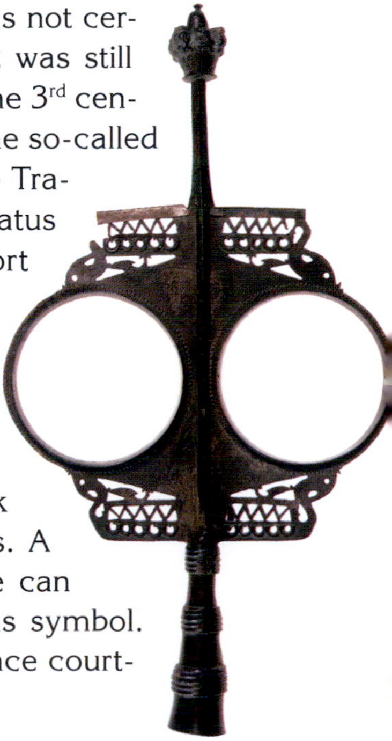

Fig. 189: Standard of a beneficiarius

ficiarii served as street police in the administration, but over time became the representative of the emperors in the provinces, coordinating imperial communication, leading imperial construction projects, and establishing themselves as part of the imperial police – to the point of spying on the inhabitants of the provinces. Whoever they were, the close connection of the owners of residential unit 2 with the imperial household still existed in the 3rd century.

The owners of residential unit 6 are also known through inscriptions and belonged to the urban elite of Ephesos. Their dedications and endowments over generations were an integral part of the urban landscape. An invocation of the god Dionysos Oreios, on the upper ledge of the back of a fountain oriented towards the peristyle courtyard (31a) of residential unit

Aptus was in charge of a cult that venerated Dionysus as the "god from the mountains and in front of the city".

Fig. 190: Inscription in the peristyle courtyard (31a) of residential unit 6 with mention of the house owner

Fig. 191: Inscription in the courtyard 36 of residential unit 6 with mention of the house owner

6, also mentions a priest, Gaius Flavius Furius Aptus, presumably the owner of the house (*fig. 190*). Aptus was in charge of a cult that venerated Dionysus as the "god from the mountains and in front of the city". In the courtyard (36), more proof for the identity of the house owner was preserved in the form of an inscription on the statue socle that flanked the steps to the

Fig. 192: Mention of the house owner C. Furius Aptus on the back side of a marble slab in Latin

> *On an inconspicuous pitcher fragment discovered during excavations in residential unit 6, the following inscription was etched: "I am the property of someone else and not of Aptus!"*

apsidal room (*fig. 191*). The life span of Gaius Flavius Furius Aptus can even be estimated –to a fairly exact degree– based on an inscription in the marble hall (31): painted dipinti feature his name in red ink on the backs of the marble panels that were delivered to the Terrace House 2 in the early Hadrianic period (*fig. 192*).

The family of the Apti was of Greek origin; the great-grandfather and grandfather had lived as indigenous Greeks with the status of peregrine until the grandfather received Roman citizenship. The conferment of Roman citizenship was the prerequisite for a Roman public career and was often connected to fast upward mobility. This was also the case with the family of Furius Aptus: his father, Titus Flavius Aristobulus, held the office of the prytanis, and he himself was probably already a member of the equestrian order because his son, Titus Flavius Lollianus Aristobulus, was the first family member to be admitted into the senatorial order. Public offices were very expensive and required an adequate financial background but also an elegant environment where the obligations of the dignitaries could be met. Residential unit 6 fulfilled the various functions of a city palace: audiences were received, celebrations took place, and the gods were honored. The close connection between business activity, patronage, hosting of guests, and religious practice inspired impressive architecture and furnishings –strongly influenced by imperial forms of representation– in the houses of the urban nobility. It is quite likely that residential unit 6 was owned by the family of the Apti up until its final destruction in the late 3rd century, because the familial inscriptions remained in place there. But not everyone or everything wanted to belong to Gaius Flavius Furius Aptus. On an inconspicuous pitcher fragment discovered during excavations in residential unit 6, the following inscription was etched: "I am the property of someone else and not of Aptus!" (*fig. 193*).

Fig. 193: Etched inscription on a pitcher fragment mentioning Aptus

Overview of Residential Units 1-7

Fig. 194: Well in the entrance area SR 1

◀ The bust of the emperor Tiberius

Residential Unit 1

*R*esidential unit 1, located in the southeast corner of Terrace House 2, was originally about 450 m² in size but also characterized by profound renovations.

The now visible remains are from AD 230 (building phase IV). Multiple older building phases, documented through excavation, reached back to the late Hellenistic period in the 1ˢᵗ century BC.

In the last imperial phase of use, the main entrance was located along stepped alley 1 and led from the higher street level (*fig. 194*) over a steep staircase into a small courtyard (SR 1), from which the central peristyle courtyard (SR 2), the rooms to the north, including a bath (SR 3-5; 7-8), and also the small latrine (SR 1a) could be reached. In addition, a staircase connected the ground level with the upper stories. Indentations caused by the door construction in the threshold illustrate that the lower and upper level could be locked separately. This detail suggests that, at least during the last building phase (around AD 260), both levels were separately rented out.

The residential unit was supplied with drinking water through two continually flowing fountains in the entrance area and the peristyle courtyard (*fig. 195*). The painted court-

Fig. 195: The peristyle courtyard SR 2

yard (SR 2) was 57 m² in size and surrounded by three corridors with mosaic floors, while the fourth corridor was rebuilt into cubicula, or small bedrooms (SR 10a and b), in the 3rd century. These were decorated with simple mosaic floors as well as wall paintings in the lesene system with emblems of erotes. Niches in the north wall were filled with sculpture, while dishes or braziers could be shown off on the built platform in room SR 10a.

A vaulted room (GEW C), designed as a reception room, was attached to the south. Its poor state of preservation only permits us to

The residential unit was supplied with drinking water through two continually flowing fountains in the entrance area and the peristyle courtyard.

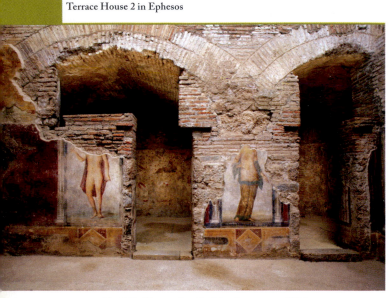

Fig. 196: The south wall of the theater room SR 6

guess at its originally rich furnishings. To the west of this vaulted room is a small latrine (SR 2a) and a stairway that led to the upper story and to the Terrace House Street.

A small and dark cubiculum (SR 11), adjoined in the west of the courtyard. To the east the courtyard, opened up onto a large, 30 m² room that has received the designation 'theater room' (SR 6) and is referred to as a triclinium (*fig. 196*). In Terrace House 2, no other room received a similarly individualistic set of images, likely selected by the patron himself. The paintings follow the three-zone system and are especially imposing due to their quality and choice of image. The main zone, above the socle, is structured by fluted columns and alternating panels of window-like views and red monochrome. Through the 'windows' are scantily clad young men and

> *To the east the courtyard, opened up onto a large, 30 m² room that has received the designation 'theater room' (SR 6) and is referred to as a triclinium.*

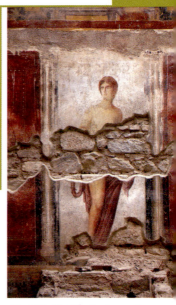

Fig. 197: The life-size figure of a female servant

girls (*figs. 197. 198*), probably understood as idealized representations of servants. They present the entering guests with small presents, flowers, garland jewelry, welcome drinks and dishes, a custom that was actually practiced during ancient feasts. They also offer up their barely covered bodies to the viewer – connotating the erotic intentionally. In the red fields small theater scenes are depicted, alternating between well-known comedies and tragedies (*fig. 199*). Of what were originally ten ancient dramas, the "Sicyonioi" by Menander and the "Oresteia" by Euripides are still preserved. Based on dipinti, or painted inscriptions, the scenes can be exactly identified. The

Fig. 198: The life-size figure of a male servant

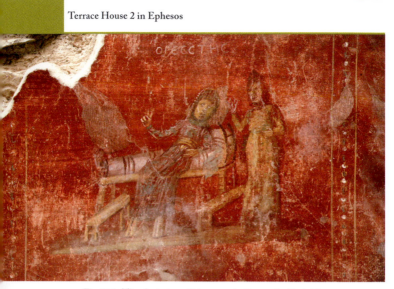

Fig. 199: The depiction of the tragedy Orestes by Euripides

> *The fate of Philoctetes, who was badly injured by a snake bite on the island of Chryse while en route to Troy.*

theatrical theme is again evoked in the upper zone by tragic theater masks in illusionistic architectural frames.

The main image occupying the north wall is a mythological scene (*fig. 200*): the fate of Philoctetes, who was badly injured by a snake bite on the island of Chryse while en route to Troy. His comrades could no longer endure his stench and screams of pain and left him behind on the island of Lemnos. After ten years of unsuccessful siege, the prophet Helenus told the Greeks that they could only win the Trojan War with the bow of Heracles. Odysseus was then assigned to find Philoctetes –who happened to have the bow in question– and bring it back to Troy. In the meantime, the dead Heracles appeared to the terminally-ill Philoctetes and promised his recovery in front of the walls of Troy. The story line and outcome are well known: the city fell, and Philoctetes was finally healed. The Philoctetes myth was picked up by numerous ancient writers, including Sophocles, Aeschylus, and also Euripides.

The image depicts the moment of the bite of the snake and the beginning of the long suffering of the collapsed hero, weakened and writhing in pain – in a way similar to the famous statue group of Laocoön. Although we do not know the exact reason for the choice of such an exceptional and unique image, we can assume that the patron consciously chose to show the suffering of Philoctetes.

Fig. 200: The depiction of the Philoctetes myth on the north wall of the theater room (SR 6)

While the reclining god Dionysus was depicted on the south wall of vault A, on vault B the goddess Aphrodite Anadyomene was shown stepping out of the sea and wringing her hair.

Two small cubicula (GEW A and B), cut into bedrock, could be entered from the so-called theater room. They were decorated with simple mosaic floors and are 10 m² and 8.5 m² in size, respectively. The wall is painted with scattered flowers in the main zone while the vaults are covered with coffer paintings. While the reclining god Dionysus was depicted on the south wall of vault A (*fig. 201*), on vault B the goddess Aphrodite Anadyomene was shown stepping out of the sea and wringing her hair. From the theater room, both gods could be viewed through the open door. Each enhances the erotic atmosphere, presenting their graceful –intentionally naked– bodies, which resonate with the young servant figures. Offering quiet retreat during the dinners in the theater room, the paintings guided the gaze and fantasy of the symposiasts.

To the north of the residential unit were the utilitarian rooms that could also be accessed through a separate entrance from stepped alley 1 (SR 4-5 and 7-8). Their simple floors were made of mud and the walls were covered with white plaster. The lack of decoration, the small room size, and also the numerous water installations suggest that these were the more functional areas of the house. Although built hearths and ovens are absent, cooking activities must have taken place here – as is indicated by the recovery of an almost complete kitchen inventory.

A distinctive feature of residential unit 1 is the 28 m² large bath (SR 3) in the northeast that was heated by a praefurnium to its north. Two building phases can be clearly differentiated: the hypocaust pillars, the floors and the tubuli of the first phase were constructed with great care. After a fire in the early 3rd century, these were hastily patched up and renovated. Instead of the elaborate marble revetment, a stucco imitation was used, and the floor of the hypocaust was not reconstructed of fine mortar but instead of rough tile meal. The bath in residential unit 1 is impressive testimony for the deteriorating economic situation of the

Fig. 201: Scatter flowers painting with the reclined god Dionysus in a cubiculum

inhabitants of the Terrace House in the course of the 3rd century AD.

Residential unit 1 holds a special position in many respects. There are comparably few finds that could be securely attributed to the imperial period. The reason for this is that large areas of the residential unit remained inhabited even after the massive destruction in the later 3rd century. The debris was removed after the catastrophe and dumped into the smaller cubicula, whose door openings were then filled. The many small cubicula on the ground level are also surprising and were constructed –instead of the large formal rooms– in the last building phase. This multiplication of smaller rooms might have been the consequence of the loss of four rooms on the ground floor of the residential unit 2, and also the transfer of the upper story to other owners or renters. The need for the lost rooms must have decisively changed the layout of the ground floor. In addition, the owning family dispensed with marble revetment and even in the 3rd century they preferred decorating their walls with paintings. It is possible that they insisted on traditional designs and rejected contemporary trends.

Residential Unit 2

To the west of residential unit 1 is residential unit 2, of about equal size (measuring 549 m^2), and located on the same terrace. Here the early imperial layout has been preserved best because only small renovations took place throughout its entire period of use and the floor levels were only slightly raised. However, the west front of the house was damaged so heavily by Byzantine building measures that its original entrance cannot be reconstructed. The main entrance to the residential unit was probably situated along stepped alley 3, where it was overbuilt in the Byzantine period by a mill room (B 16).

From this presumed entrance, you could reach a small courtyard (SR 27) with four columns from where the nearby utility rooms (SR 27b and c, SR 30) and the small latrine SR 29 could be accessed (*fig. 202*). Originally the kitchen (SR 27a) adjoined this space to the north, but it was later moved to the south side where it can still be clearly recognized based on a wall installation. From the courtyard it was also possible to enter the large, central peristyle courtyard (SR 22/23) that was 148 m^2 in size and originally had nine monolithic white columns embellished with Corinthian capitals (*fig. 203*). The still-visible row of columns in the south, carrying the arcades, was

It is possible that they insisted on traditional designs and rejected contemporary trends.

Fig. 202: The entrance courtyard SR 27

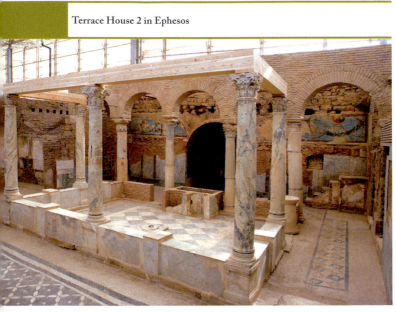

Fig. 203: The peristyle courtyard SR 22/23

made of spolia in the Late Antique to early Byzantine period. The impluvium was surrounded on all four sides by a medium-high parapet wall and corridors lined with mosaic floors. A flowing fountain in the south and an additional decorative fountain supplied sufficient amounts of water. The socle and main zone of the walls of the courtyard are revetted with polychrome marble slabs while the upper zone was painted with erotes-garlands on a blue background. In the southwest corner, a staircase provided access the upper story of the residential unit, and immediately beside it, a Heros-Equitans relief depicting a heroic rider was set deep into the south wall.

The exedra in the south (GEW D) was probably intended to capture the attention of the visitor. It was cut into the bedrock and was intricately furnished (*fig. 204*). Guests

The exedra in the south (GEW D) was probably intended to capture the attention of the visitor.

Fig. 204: The exedra with rich mosaic décor

were possibly received here and precious items could be ostentatiously put on display. Glass mosaics decorated the vault and lunette, while the walls and the floor were covered with multi-colored stones and marble. The central medallion of the vault mosaic shows the divine couple Dionysus and Ariadne embedded in an illusionary vineyard, a heavenly paradise. In the lunette, two peacocks are facing each other and a basket filled with fruit is set between them. In front of the exedra was a southern walkway with a figural floor mosaic: a procession, or sea thiasos, is framed by a guilloche which illustrates Amphitrite, Triton and a hippocamp (*fig. 205*). The elaborate furnishing of the exedra deliberately emphasizes the function of the peristyle courtyard as the center of communication of the house and as the entrance area.

Fig. 205: The Amphitrite mosaic in front of the exedra

The rooms to the east of the peristyle court-yard had a formal function, as can be seen in their decorations of figural wall paintings (room of the muses, SR 19/20) or of sculptural stucco (SR 17). The rooms in the west (SR 25 and 26), however, can be identified as private spaces. The walls of these small cellae were decorated with paintings in the lesene-

system or with scattered flowers, and the floor covered with mosaic. A small, indirectly lighted room (SR 12) with a mud floor was probably used for storage.

It is possible that room SR 18, 14 m² in size, or its equivalent on the second floor, was exquisitely decorated. In the destruction debris, numerous small statuettes of marble or colored stone as well as ivory were found lying on the mosaic floor, among them the so-called ivory frieze (*fig. 206*). On this 20 cm high, 108 cm long frieze, the emperor Trajan with his retinue and a delegation of barbarians are depicted as almost fully-rounded figures. Three scenes divided by victories were originally included in the architectural, wooden frame, as were two caryatids along the side,

Fig. 206: The large ivory frieze, found in room SR 18

possibly personifications of the provinces Armenia and Arabia. As with many other pieces of moveable inventory, it cannot be determined whether the ivory pieces came from the first or second floor. In any case, the mosaics and wall paintings as well as the finds from the debris suggest that the upper story was elaborately decorated, probably not only used by the family but also functioned as an area where guests were hosted.

In the north, by the peristyle courtyard SR 22/23, two additional rooms (SR 24 and 28) were probably also used for the reception of guests and measured respectively 35.5 m² and 31.5 m² in size. They communicated with the courtyard through wide door and window openings and offered charming visual site lines (*fig. 207*). The parallel design is engaging, particularly when the exedra in the peristyle courtyard is compared with room SR 24, where the fountain niche on the side exactly mirrors the wall and vault décor of the exedra (*fig. 208*). Above the marble revetment of

Fig. 207: The triclinium SR 24 with fountain and platform

Above the marble revetment of the fountain wall, glass mosaics with alluring water nymphs decorate small apses.

Fig. 208: A spring nymph on a mosaic in the fountain niche

the fountain wall, glass mosaics with alluring water nymphs decorate small apses. The mosaic floor reflects the position of actual klinai, and a built platform as well as fittings found from tables and klinai and can thus be associated with hosting and dining with guests. Both rooms served the social needs of the patron to flaunt his status, as is demonstrated by multiple private portraits in marble and ivory that probably depicted family members.

A unique feature of residential unit 2 is that it was almost completely sealed by a massive layer of debris that included numerous decorative elements. This makes it possible to reconstruct a large part of the original content of the household, including precious items, as for example the statuette of an Egyptian priest, and items of daily use such as oil lamps and unguents, small oil flasks.

Residential Unit 3
Originally there were two comparably-sized residential units on the middle of the three hillside terraces. The western unit was di-

In the south was an originally elongated room (16a) that was divided into two equally-sized rooms of 8-9 m² in building phase IV.

vided into two separate houses in the course of the 2nd century. In result, residential unit 3 is the smallest in Terrace House 2 at 260 m², but is also in no way inferior due to its exquisite furnishings (*fig. 209*).

The entrance was – similar to that of residential unit 2– in the west, but it was completely overbuilt by the construction of a 26.5 m² mill room (B 17). The columned central peristyle courtyard (16b) was reached through a small entrance area and was surrounded on three sides by very narrow corridors. In the south was an originally elongated room (16a) that was divided into

Fig. 209: View of residential unit 3

two equally-sized rooms of 8-9 m² in building phase IV (around AD 230). Despite their small size, both rooms featured high-quality mosaic décor with central motifs showing the busts of the god Dionysus and of Medusa (*fig. 210*). Three layers of wall painting illustrate the changing history of the design: on the bottom layer is the scattered-flowers-motif from building phase II (about AD 120), above that the lesene-system with animal emblems from phase III (around AD 150), and finally, a painted marble imitation from phase IV (around AD 230).

The formal rooms were located in the north (17), the east (12), and also to the west (B17), but the last is almost entirely destroyed by the Byzantine construction measures. The so-called lion room (17) to their north is about 20 m² in size. It is named after its floor mosaic (*fig. 211*) that is contemporary with the wall painting of birds in a lesene-system from

Fig. 210: The mosaics in the room 16a with Dionysus and Medusa as central emblems

Fig. 211: The lion mosaic from room 17

building phase III (around AD 150).

The most stately and largest room of residential unit 3 is located to the southeast of the peristyle courtyard. The 31.5 m² large room is the so-called room of the muses (12). The wall paintings were executed around AD 230, after the walls had been badly deformed, and they starkly contrast in quality and execution with the flooring of simple square tiles. Above a meander socle with green cruciform flowers is the usual lesene-system. As central motifs, the nine muses who were considered the patron goddess of the arts, are depicted with naming inscriptions: Clio, Euterpe, Thalia, Melpomene, Terpsichore, Erato, Polyhymnia, Urania, and Calliope (*fig. 212*). They carry musical instruments or similar attributes that signify their respective art. The poet Sappho, who died around AD 570, was added to this scheme, since she was considered the tenth muse in antiquity. The central place in the middle of the south wall is held by Apollo Musagetes, the god of music, song, and poetry, and leader of the muses. The upper zone

> *They carry musical instruments or similar attributes that signify their respective art.*

is decorated with architectural painting that has only been well-preserved in the south. In the center a theater scene is still recognizable with two –probably bronze– statues of naked male heroes, holding shield and lance on either side.

It is likely that residential unit 3 also had an upper story, but it is more difficult to localize the industrial areas of the house. Due to the far-reaching Byzantine interference and the erosion of the slope, the areas in the west and northwest are badly damaged and do not allow for any reconstruction of the original lay-

Fig. 212: The south wall of the room of the muses

> *The reception rooms were again situated in the north, of which the 23 m² large room to the east (25) was decorated with unusual stucco that imitated marble.*

out of the rooms. In analogy with residential unit 2, it is likely that the utility areas of the house as well as the latrine were located in this area.

The owners of residential unit 3 attached great value to the room design and furnishings despite the small size of the house. The mosaic decorations as well as the wall paintings belong to some of the most exquisite in the entirety of Terrace House 2. The existence of at least three figural mosaics might reflect the unique preference and personal taste of the family and would have been a considerable financial expenditure. The findings show that despite a small living area, we cannot assume that the furnishings were simple or that the owner was financially lacking.

Residential Unit 5

In the 2nd century AD, residential units 3 and 5, originally connected, were separated into individual houses. A long corridor connected the center of residential unit 5 with the entrance on the stepped alley 3. At the center of the house was a peristyle courtyard (24) with six columns that had ionic capitals and measured about 64 m². The courtyard is surrounded by ambulatories on three sides, and in the south a large exedra (13) with marble revetment opens up onto the courtyard and is almost of the same width as the courtyard (*fig. 213*). In the final building phase (IV, around AD 230), the peristyle courtyard was revetted with marble that covered the older paintings, and decorated with an attractive fountain ensemble in the south-west corner that reinforced a comfortable room climate and also provided sufficient drinking water.

The reception rooms were again situated in the north, of which the 23 m² large room to the east (25) was decorated with unusual stucco that imitated marble (*see fig. 111*). Above a green socle are rectangular dark red panels with white frames. The contemporary marble floor matched the design of the walls and matched their color composition. The western adjoining room (26), 21.5 m² size, was once heated, as indicated by the installation of a

Fig. 213: View of residential unit 5

praefurnium and suspensura. Furthermore it had marble revetted floors and walls, a fountain along the south wall, as well as a water drain in the floor; its function as a bath cannot be dismissed. This probably was a warm reception room where it was possible to receive and host guests even in the cold seasons.

Simple furnishings are found in a small cubiculum (12a) to the east of the peristyle courtyard with a simple white mosaic floor and wall paintings imitating marble. Another reception room in the west, 13 m² in size, was more carefully decorated and is known as the so-called erotes room (18). Flying erotes appear here as emblems in the main zone; of these, some play musical instruments, some offer guests drinks or flowers (*fig. 214*). From the corridor it was possible to reach a richly-decorated upper story of the apartment over a staircase (*fig. 215*) that also cut into the erotes room. A room of the muses was located in the upper story as the numerous wall painting fragments discovered in the debris suggest.

Despite its small living space, all of the characteristic room types are represented in residential unit 5. These include the exedra in the south, the re-

Fig. 214: A serving Eros

Fig. 215: The staircase to the upper story of the residential unit 5

ception rooms, multiple cubicula of varying quality, as well as a richly-furnished second story. The interior decoration of the house, with marble and mosaic floors, walls painted and revetted with marble, as well as decorative fountains and other furnishings, are unmistakable signs of an elevated standard of living with a distinct need for self-representation. But in the first and second stories, there is no evidence for utility rooms or a latrine or kitchen. These were probably located in the west of the residential unit where the Byzantine building activities resulted in considerable changes.

Flying erotes appear here as emblems in the main zone; of these, some play musical instruments, some offer guests drinks or flowers.

Terrace House 2 in Ephesos

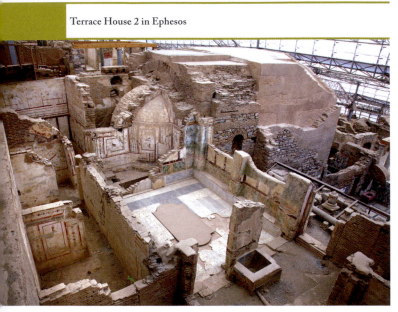

Fig. 216: View of residential unit 4

The central pillar courtyard (21), 55 m² in size, was originally furnished with columns and a decorative fountain.

Residential Unit 4

The eastern half of the central terrace is occupied by residential unit 4, which is 3.5 m lower than residential units 3 and 5. The appearance of the house today, circa 203 m² in size, is quite a bit different from its early imperial design of 450 m², because its entire north area was gradually incorporated into residential unit 6 (*fig. 216*).

The entrance to the house was situated along the stepped alley 1 and was highlighted by an entrance with marble revetment. A second staircase, that could also be entered separately from outside, led to both upper stories. The entrance area (4) directly connected with the industrial areas of the house (14); additionally, there was a room for the house cult (5) as well as a latrine (4a) carved into the rock.

The central pillar courtyard (21), 55 m² in size, was originally furnished with columns and a decorative fountain, while in the walkway was the (already mentioned) painting of Socrates and Urania on a red background, above them the mythological frieze of the discovery of Achilles on Scyros. But the peristyle courtyard was completely renovated (*fig. 217*): around AD 150 (building phase III), the columns were replaced with pillars and from the courtyard the freshly applied garden paintings gave the impression of an illusionary view of nature. In building phase IV (around AD 230), the basin was abandoned

Fig. 217: The courtyard (21) in residential unit 4

and the garden paintings were replaced by attractive marble imitation. In the south the former walkway was already surrendered to residential unit 6 by around AD 150, when the large apsidal hall (8) was built. The small rooms (14a-d) were created at the same time and the two middle rooms (14b and c) can be identified as klinai rooms. Behind them were small storage rooms carved into the rock.

The renovations resulted in a complete re-furnishing: not only the courtyard (21), but also the rooms in the west (15) were covered with elaborate marble imitation and above them architectural painting on a white background. The side rooms were decorated with scattered flowers with integrated garlands and birds. The utility room (22) received a décor in the lesene-system with emblems of hunting dogs, an ibex (*fig. 218*), and hunting erotes. From here a staircase led down into a heating room that heated the apsidal hall (8) of residential unit 6. A pictorial program can only be recognized in the large north room (7). It measures 28.5 m^2 and is a room of the muses, so popular in the 3rd century. As a particularly exquisite accessory, a statuette of Artemis was set up in a niche in the west wall and was decorated with painted scattered flowers.

Residential unit 4 had two richly-furnished upper stories. At least for the second floor, a columned courtyard with marble revetment and two main rooms have been verified that would have provided good prerequisites for the reception and hosting of guests. The fur-

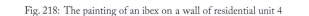

Fig. 218: The painting of an ibex on a wall of residential unit 4

nishing starkly contrasts with that of the first floor, where marble revetments and mosaic floors are lacking.

The construction of the marble hall (31) and the apsidal hall (8) in residential unit 6 were large structural measures that greatly affected residential unit 4 and probably were the result of changed ownership. At least the ground floor of residential unit 4 was –spatially and functionally– closely connected with the urban palais in the north, residential unit 6, while the upper stories could have been used as separate units.

Residential Unit 6
Residential unit 6 was located in the northeast of Terrace House 2 on the lowest northern terrace.

Residential unit 4 had two richly-furnished upper stories.

In the course of the 2nd century AD, a generous and magnificently designed city palais came into being (*fig. 219*) when the originally 620 m² large residential unit was expanded to the south and was entirely altered by the construction of the so-called marble hall (31) and the large, so-called 'basilica' or apsidal hall (8).

The great house now covered 950 m² and could be directly entered form the Curetes Street, from where a staircase led up to the peristyle courtyard (31a) with twelve columns (*fig. 220*). It was impressive due to its dimensions (251.5 m²), its multiple stories, as well as its luxurious furnishings. Similar to other formal rooms of the residential units, the floors and walls of the courtyard were revetted with marble. The large columns had Corinthian composite capitals that carried wooden architraves. In the north, adjoining the entrance area in the west, was a 25.5 m² large room (31b)

Fig. 219: A view of residential unit 6

Fig. 220: The large peristyle courtyard (31a) of residential unit 6

that opened up onto the courtyard at nearly its entire width. A built-in aedicula with columns and traces of wall cupboards suggest that the family archive and a library was stored here, and also that family cult rituals took place here. The west front of the large peristyle courtyard (31a) bordered other formal, partially-heated rooms (36c-e) that originally opened up onto the courtyard like an exedra, but in building phase IV (around AD 230), this was functionally changed (36e) or closed (36d). Room 42, to the northwest of the residential unit, was redesigned in building phase II (around AD 120)

The large columns had Corinthian composite capitals that carried wooden architraves.

From the southern walkway, the so-called marble hall (31) could be entered, which was a magnificent 178 m² large room.

with wall paintings influenced by individualizing and uniquely western models, though its floor followed the typical, local carpet style. In building phase II, a multi-room bathing complex (M1-3) was incorporated into the former eastern walkway of the peristyle courtyard. The entrance was in the south and opened up onto the peristyle with large, arched glass windows. In the course of the renovation phase, the southern walkway was separated from the courtyard with parapet walls and latticework as well as marble portals. The latrine, revetted in marble, was located at the western end of the corridor, as was a staircase that led up into

Fig. 221: View of the marble hall (31)

the first floor of the residential unit in building phase IV (after AD 230).

The large formal rooms were situated to the south of the peristyle courtyard. From the southern walkway, the so-called marble hall (31) could be entered, which was a magnificent 178 m² large room (*fig. 221*). It was lavishly furnished in the early Hadrianic period, after AD 121, and remained almost unchanged until its final destruction in the third quarter of the 3rd century. The marble hall was used for receptions and banquets and provided enough space for at least nine wide klinai, each of which could fit three reclining people (*fig. 222*). In this luxurious environment, the elite of the city probably met for social events. The furnishings of the room are very precious and expensive: marble revetment was prominent on the floors and walls and the placement of the klinai was emphasized by a black-and-white mosaic strip. A centrally-aligned jet

Fig. 222: The reconstruction of the marble hall (31)

Fig. 223: A polychrome and artistically decorated opus sectile slab

fountain and an additional decorative fountain, integrated into the south wall and supplied with fresh water by a canal, not only enhanced the environment of the room but also created an elegant surrounding. A wooden ceiling covered the room and was decorated with gilded and carved décor. The walls were revetted in three zones with partially polychrome marble slabs and opus sectile fields (*fig. 223*). In addition to vegetal decorative systems, some figural images are preserved (*fig. 224*).

To the west of the so-called marble hall followed further large, formal rooms. A large courtyard (36) measuring 58 m² could be entered from the marble hall as well as from

Fig. 224: The reconstruction of the north wall and the ceiling of the marble hall (31)

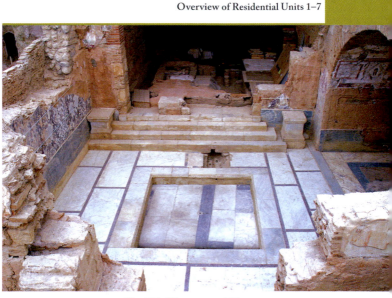

Fig. 225: The courtyard 36

the south corridor. It had a deep impluvium that was covered by a groin vault following building phase III (around AD 150) and was lighted through a round opening in the ceiling (*fig. 225*). The apsidal hall (8), 80 m² in size, adjoined in the south and could be entered through a staircase that was framed by Aphrodite statues. Originally this room was also richly decorated with rich marble revetments and glass mosaics and functioned as a

A wooden ceiling covered the room and was decorated with gilded and carved décor. The walls were revetted in three zones with partially polychrome marble slabs and opus sectile fields.

Fig. 226: The decorated ceiling of the stucco room (8a)

A door was placed into the west wall that was straddled by an arch and led into a small room, only 18 m² large but very elaborately decorated.

room for hosting guests and banquets. A basin installed in the hall and supplied with fresh water –possibly for holding fish for decoration and eating– was removed around AD 230 for a heating system linked to that in the south.

A door was placed into the west wall that was straddled by an arch and led into a small room, only 18 m² large but very elaborately decorated: the stucco room (8a), which was reserved for private meetings of close friends and cult rituals (*fig. 226*). On three sides, high niches were set into the walls –either revetted with marble or painted with marble imitation– where statuettes or cult objects were set. A stucco coffer vault covered the room. The emblems in the geometrically framed fields reflect a Dionysiac theme and show masks, satyrs, centaurs, as well as lions and goats. The lunette, the field below the vault, was originally filled by a figural couple that is sadly only preserved in silhouette: framed by erotes, the divine couple Aphrodite and Dionysus once faced each other (*fig. 227*).

Fig. 227: The lunette of the stucco room (8a) with the depiction of the divine couple Dionysus and Aphrodite

Another elaborately decorated formal room (36a) opens up onto the courtyard 36 in its full width (*fig. 228*). Floors and walls are covered with marble slabs, the vault is painted with an intricate erotes-garland-frieze on a

Fig. 228: The vaulted room 36a

Fig. 229: The painted ceiling in room 36a

Due to its dimensions and architectural design, residential unit 6 goes beyond the scope of a private urban house and instead follows imperial palatial architecture.

white background, and architectural painting is added above in the lunette (*fig. 229*); two openings in the ceiling provided lighting. The freshwater basin built into the north wall of the room could have been used for holding fish for decorative and or edible purposes (*fig. 230*). From the courtyard (36), a staircase (32a) led up into the first floor of the apartment, where additional richly furnished rooms were located. While the first floor of the residential unit appears to be lacking a kitchen and other industrial areas and was solely used for representation, the second story does appear to have included the utility areas.

Due to its dimensions and architectural design, residential unit 6 goes beyond the scope of a private urban house and instead follows imperial palatial architecture. The individual room types and also their sequence suggest that this was the city residence of an Ephesian dignitary and a space for his political and social activities. We are fortunate to be able to study not only the house itself, but also to be able to trace the owner's family over the course of multiple generations. We can therefore exactly attribute the house: it is the urban residence of the family of Gaius Flavius Furius Aptus and was used for the reception of his clients, commercial and political meetings, and also for the reception and hosting of his guests.

Fig. 230: The fish basin in room 36a

Terrace House 2 in Ephesos

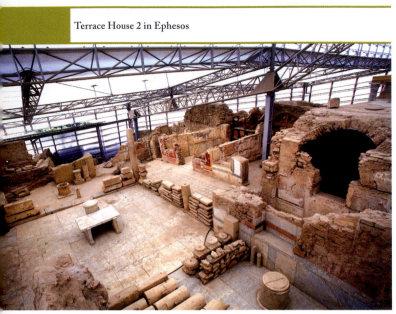

Fig. 231: View of residential unit 7

The center of the house was formed by a 143 m² large peristyle (38b) with eight columns and Doric capitals.

The phenomenon of a deliberate adoption of imperial palatial architecture and its adaptation in the private house can be clearly illustrated in residential unit 6. This not only concerns the architecture of the city palace of the Apti, but also its interior design. As a family of equestrian and later senatorial status, they were well-aware of the palaces in Roman Italy. It is not surprising that the closest parallels for the Ephesian city palace can be found in the imperial palaces of Rome as well as in Hadrian's villa at Tivoli.

Residential Unit 7

Residential unit 7 covers an area of about 520 m² in the northwest part of the insula, on the lowest northern terrace (*fig. 231*). Here also the original entrance situation cannot be exactly reconstructed due to extensive Byzantine building activities, but it is likely that the building was entered over stepped alley 3.

Fig. 232: A niche in the exedra of residential unit 7

The center of the house was formed by a 143 m² large peristyle (38b) with eight columns and Doric capitals. It was surrounded in the west, north and south by a corridor covered with a marble floor. In the south was a large, marble revetted room (38), about 35 m², that opened up onto the courtyard, exedra-like, in its entire width. A large niche was set into the center of the south wall (*fig. 232*) that provided space

Fig. 233: The bust of the emperor Tiberius

to display sculpture. At the time of the final destruction, a bust of the emperor Tiberius (AD 14-37) and his mother Livia, as well as the bronze sculpture of a snake (*figs. 233. 234. 235*) were on display here. In the courtyard and exedra, two puteal wellheads were built around deep wells that served as back-up water reservoirs should the urban water supply fail. Across from the entrance in the east, multiple rooms with upscale furnishings opened up onto the courtyard, and in the north a small bathing complex (38e and h) was added in building phase II (around AD 120). The side rooms and industrial areas, especially the latrine, were probably located in the west, immediately beside

Fig. 234: The bust of the empress Livia

Fig. 235: Bronze snake from room 38

From the peristyle courtyard, a steep staircase led up to the second floor where the industrial areas were located, including a large latrine (34/34a).

the entrance, but this cannot be proven due to later Byzantine constructions. From the peristyle courtyard, a steep staircase led up to the second floor where the industrial areas were located, including a large latrine (34/34a). In the course of the large renovations in building phase II (around AD 120), a peristyle courtyard (32c/d) was built in the east part of the upper story and led into other living quarters. Architecture linking residential units 6 and 7 has also been discovered.

Residential unit 7 holds a special role in the study of Terrace House 2 because the

Fig. 236: Traces of soot in room 38d of residential unit 7

The mills were supplied with water from the Değirmendere aqueduct that filled a 12.5 m² large reservoir (SR 30) located in the southwest of Terrace House 2.

massive earthquake destruction can be documented here: the columns in the peristyle courtyard had fallen over and broken on a layer of ash and also showed clear traces of fire (*fig. 236*). The earthquake destructions are particularly impressive in the rooms to the east: the mosaic floor of the room (38d) has clear tears that were caused by horizontal shifts, is quite deformed and its surface is formed like waves. The north wall was able to withstand the pressure but the marble revetment was broken. Suggest an earthquake with subsequent fire, the paintings of the north wall were badly burned. Destruction traces on the south wall also are typical of an earthquake, where the walls buckled and partially shifted against the slope to the south. These clear indications of an earthquake are important criteria –in combination with the coins discovered in the peristyle courtyard– for the temporal classification and evaluation of the catastrophic destruction that led to the entire abandonment of Terrace House 2.

The Late Antique-Early Byzantine Workshops

After the destruction of the Roman houses, in Late Antiquity an extensive workshop district developed in the western part of Terrace House 2. Potteries, workshops for metals, an operation for processing stones, as well as a large mill complex were spread across the entire area.

The mill complex consisted of eight water wheel courses that negotiated a difference in height of 25 m. The system was built in three phases: the most prominent mill along the Curetes Street, between the Octagon and Heroon, is surprisingly also the oldest. Later, the mill row was expanded to the south and two further chambers (41c and 46) were constructed. In the last expansion phase in the late 6th century AD, four additional chambers (B 16, 17, 18, 44) and the stone saw complex were added in the northwest.

The mills were supplied with water from the Değirmendere aqueduct that filled a 12.5 m^2 large reservoir (SR 30) located in the southwest of Terrace House 2. This provided the constant water pressure necessary for a well-functioning mill operation.

The 40 cm wide and 30 cm deep courses, with an average slope of 2-3 degrees, were partially set into old walls while some new canals were also built. These are clearly grain mills, fed by water of the early Byzantine period (*fig. 237*). Since grain has a longer shelf life than flour, the milling processes only took place when needed and as close to the final use as possible. Therefore, it is not surprising to find this pre-industrial mill complex so

In the early 7th century, the mill complex on top of Terrace House 2 could supply 8,000-12,000 people with flour when in continuous use for 12 hours.

Fig. 237: Reconstruction of a Byzantine mill

close to the core of the city; possible noise and dust pollution was probably accepted because it secured the supply.

Due to the sinter deposits, it has been possible to reconstruct both overshot wheels and midshot water wheels of wood. The actual mills were located in closed chambers where in the bottom half the horizontal energy is converted into a vertical turning motion while the actual grain mills were set up in the upper part of the chamber. Numerous fragments of the mill stones have been preserved. In the early 7th century, the mill complex on top of Terrace House 2 could supply 8,000-12,000 people with flour –the staple food– when in continuous use for 12 hours.

A two-room workshop where stone was processed developed in the northeast of the complex (*fig. 238*). At the center of the complex was a stone saw machine 3 × 8.5 m in size that was used to cut marble slabs. The revetment of floors but especially of walls with marble was still popular in the early Byzantine period. Spectacular evidence for this is found in private houses and public buildings, especially in the churches.

The machine was operated by a large backshot water wheel with a diameter of 2.8 m and a width of 65 cm. Through a crank shaft, the circular motion of the wheel was converted into a horizontal thrust. The saw itself was harnessed into a frame, a head saw, that again was mounted to a wood contraption and weighted down in order to produce a vertical cut. Two *in situ* ashlar-like sawing pieces

The location of the stone saw is almost perfect. The water supply through the mill course was secured and the transport routes for the necessary raw materials were limited.

demonstrate that, per frame, two parallel iron saw blades were inserted with a length of 2 m and a height of 8 cm. During the sawing process, a constant flow of water and silica sand were necessary. The water was directly channeled in over wooden chutes and flushed the sands in and out and also was needed for the cooling of the cutting process. The sand, the actual abrasive, had to be added by hand. The slabs were not fully cut to prevent their falling; instead, a socle of about 1-2 cm was left over and the slabs were then broken off. When the slabs were cut, they were further processed on site. In multiple workstations close by, they were first sanded down but the slabs did not receive their final polish until after they were mounted.

The location of the stone saw is almost perfect. The water supply through the mill course was secured and the transport routes for the necessary raw materials were limited. The former Roman city center of Ephesos was filled with marble buildings and their building elements lent themselves for further processing. Without much effort, the elements were brought to the stone saw. Unfinished or semi-finished pieces of Byzantine architectural sculpture were found in the workshop. For the production of four slabs, cut out of marble block 80 cm high and about 10 cm wide, 10 days of 12 hours of labor were necessary. The stone saw would have been capable of cutting 330 m^2 of slabs per year.

The late antique-early Byzantine workshop area above Terrace House 2 has been under scientific study by experts of the Römisch-Germanisches Zentralmuseum in Mainz since 2005.

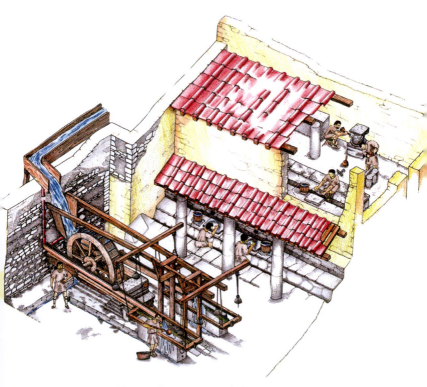

Fig. 238: Reconstruction of a Byzantine stone saw

Self-Guided Tour of Terrace House 2

(Fig. 239)

Multi-layer wallpaintings in residential unit 3

Terrace House 2, a city block covering an area of about 4,000 m², consists of a total of seven houses that are referred to by specialists as 'residential units'.

The luxurious houses were constructed in the Tiberian period (AD 25-50) and remained in use until the late 3rd century, when they were completely destroyed by an earthquake between AD 270 and 280.

When entering Terrace House 2, make sure to take a glance to the south. Here you will see the back wall of a Hellenistic fountain house (3rd-1st century BC) that extends into a later tavern. The water flowed out of the lion gargoyles, of which two are still *in situ.*

To the right of the ticket booth, a row of tavernas are visible to the west that open up onto the Curetes Street. Up the steep staircase, you will reach viewing location 1. To the right, the original staircase to residential unit 6 is still visible: a couple steps with marble revetment are preserved.

Viewing Location 1

The first viewing location offers an impressive view into the open peristyle courtyard (room 31a) of residential unit 6 with its re-erected columns (4×4). Above the massive monolithic columns are Corinthian composite capitals; the wooden architrave is a modern addition. In the last building phase (around AD 260), the courtyard was three stories high. Both the courtyard and the ambulatories are furnished with mosaic floors; on the balustrade of medium height in the south, a Greek inscription can be found in middle of the upper ledge. This is an invocation of the god Dionysus which also refers to the owner of the house, a certain Gaius Flavius Furius Aptus. Only the iron dowels remain of the statue of the god originally installed in this place. Adjoining rooms located on the west and north ambulatories were rooms of formal character, and opened up onto the courtyard through doors or windows.

A room in the north (31b), decorated with wall paintings and floor mosaics, deserves a better look: a small aedicula is set in the center of the north wall and held up by columns and pilasters. The entire wall to the right and left was covered by a wooden cupboard for the storage of scrolls and in the west a long bench offered a place to sit. A wide multi-paneled folding door was attached to the threshold facing the courtyard. It is likely that this was a room reserved for cult rituals with an adjacent library, possibly even the family archive. The rooms to the west (36c-e) were revetted with marble; the slabs have either remained *in situ* or their imprints in the mortar are still visible. The holes for the ceiling beams of wood and the remains of the flooring level from the second story can also be easily recognized here. If you look closely, you will find a cascade fountain revetted with marble above room 36d.

From viewing location 1, you will enter a small, multi-chamber bath complex (M1-3) that was entered from the south in antiquity. When the bath was relinquished and repurposed as a storage area, the corridor –still in use in the north– was created. The bathing complex was installed in the early 2ⁿᵈ century AD in the east walkway of the peristyle courtyard and was repeatedly changed. In the first room you can still study the ancient wall heating system on the floor: along the walls, a row of hollow tiles (tubuli) were mounted on a thick layer of mortar, and another layer of mortar with tile meal, frequently used for mounting marble slabs due to its fast drying properties, was added on top of that. Additionally, there was a hypocaust constructed under the floor, where the hot air was evenly dispersed in the room.

In the two next rooms (M1-2), a look upwards will reward you with a completely preserved flat groin vault. It consists of upright standing tiles and in the corner a flue pipe is sticking out of the wall-floor-heating system. A well niche is visible in the east wall of room M1. Both rooms opened up to the west onto the peristyle courtyard with wide glass windows. These openings were later walled up, but the original width of the windows can be estimated by the joint in the west wall.

Room M3 adjoins in the south and is filled by two large basins. A tile arch construction in the east wall accents the basin, lined with marble slabs, located. The water spout –a lead pipe– which collected overflowing water from the basin in a gutter is still preserved. The apse is charmingly designed, including a large, white shell formed in stucco on a blue background. The large western basin reaches into the peristyle courtyard and was connected with it through three glass windows. These basins were also lined with marble; a step on the inside aided entering bathers.

On the north wall of the room you will see that the entrance to room M 2 was originally much wider but was later narrowed down. From here you will enter the south walkway of the peristyle courtyard through a marble portal.

Viewing Location 2

First take a look back into the peristyle courtyard (31a) as it appeared in its last phase, with ambulatories on three sides –of which the southern one was separated from the rest by a portal– with a bathing complex in the east as well as formal rooms in the west and north. The view into room 36c shows the high-quality marble wall revetment as well as the niche located higher up on the east wall.

In the south you will find a large dining room, the so-called marble hall (31), that measures 178 m². It was entered through a wide door. Traces of the mountings for the door hinges still remain. The current appearance reflects an expansion phase of the 2nd century AD, since the room used to be a lot smaller. On the east wall, you can see a refilled break where the original south wall was located. The hall was covered by a marble slab floor and a wide u-shaped panel of mosaic stones where the klinai (dining couches) were set up.

The wall decoration was particularly grand and divided into four zones. The socle zone consists of 1 cm thin slabs of cippollino verde, a colored marble of the island Euboea. Many slabs were cut from the same block and then juxtaposed in mirror reversal when mounted to the walls. Pilasters with exceptionally high-quality capitals frame the main zone. Elongated areas with narrow frames were set between the pilasters. The marble used for this, the Phrygian pavonazzetto, came from the imperial quarries in Dokimeion. The once-attached slabs can still be recognized by their deep impression in the mortar. Another decorative zone was located above the marble slab décor and consisted of geometric and figural opus sectile designs. Except for the impressions in the mortar, only a few remains of the white marble frame have been preserved in the southeast corner of the room. A painted zone completed the upper edge of the wall decoration. We must also imagine a decorated and gilded wood ceiling that covered the entire wall as well as windows along the walls.

A fountain with marble revetment was set into the south wall and a glass mosaic was integrated into the niche. It was fed by a canal and provided constant fresh water. In the front part of the room was a jet fountain set in alabaster: a high and twisted stand is evidence of its decorative basin. From the marble hall a narrow corridor led to the bath (M1-3) in the east walkway of the courtyard as well as to the courtyard (36) adjoining in the west.

When you return to the south walkway (31a), take a minute to look at the floor a bit more closely. It is a mosaic typical of Terrace House 2, with geometric decoration in dark gray, white, and yellow-red. Canals are located under the patch of marble slabs that drained off the waste water. For example, a downspout projecting from the southwest corner of the corridor directed the runoff water from the roof. The south wall of the corridor makes an allowance for a deep well supplying ground water; this was probably already located here in the Hellenistic period but continued to be used in the Roman imperial period. The walls are revetted with marble slabs and the upper zone is decorated with fine architectural paintings. A latrine (36L) is located at the west end of the corridor, its floor and walls covered with marble. Running water was part of its luxurious design and immediately washed away all excrement.

Immediately beside the latrine, a staircase (36b) led to the upper story. While the lower steps have been completely preserved, only the impressions of the upper ones can be seen in the plaster of the wall paintings. The staircase was decorated with marble imitation and in the upper zone with architectural painting. Three aediculae can be seen on a white background with candelabras set into the two outer aedicula. Green, leafy garlands are attached to the candelabras and wound around a vessel set into the middle, higher aedicula. Leave the south corridor and climb two steps to enter the courtyard (36).

Viewing Location 3

The almost-square courtyard (36) was the center of the house from which all other parts of the house could be accessed. At its center is a deep impluvium that is fully lined with slabs of alabaster and was necessary for the drainage of rainwater. The drainage outlets, directly connected to the canals below, are still visible. The floor and the lower zone of the wall decoration are furnished with marble slabs, but on the west wall imitation marble paintings are affixed instead of real marble. The courtyard received a groin vault in building phase III (around AD 150); all four corners are still preserved. In the center of the ceiling you must imagine a round light opening, an oculus. The upper zone of the walls and the vault itself are covered by a delicate architectural painting that can be studied particularly well on the north wall and in the northwest corner.

Two rooms are accessible through the court-yard: the large apsidal hall (8), 80 m² in size, and the exedra-like vaulted room (36a) in the west. The apsidal hall (8) was entered over four, wide stairs and could be closed off by a multi-part door. The entire arch was closed off by a window. To the right and left of the entrance were bases for two statues that were probably representations of the goddess Aphrodite, based on the inscriptions. On the right base the owner of the house, Gaius Furius Aptus, is again mentioned.

The current state of preservation is deceptive, since this hall was once splendidly decorated: floors and walls were covered by marble slabs, above which was a painted frieze of which a few fragments are still preserved (in the western spring of the vault), and the large apse was furnished with a glass mosaic. At the time of the construction of the apsidal hall, around AD 150, a large basin was set into the ground in the northern half of the room that was constantly supplied with fresh water through a canal. After a complete redesign around AD 230, the basin was removed and a floor heating system installed in the entire room. The furnace room, the praefurnium, is located in the crown of the apse under floor level (8c). The brick relieving arch for the praefurnium is visible above the actual furnace channel. A narrow doorway in the south leads into another side room (8b) that was probably used for storage.

Another small room (8a) had a completely different function and was entered through a door in the west wall of the apsidal hall. This is the so-called stucco room, which received its name thanks to its exceptional and exquisite interior decoration. The large apsidal hall was likely an audience and banquet room while the small and dimly lighted stucco room might have been used for private meetings and rituals of the house cult.

The second room (36a) accessible from the courtyard was located in the west and was partially cut out of the rock: the green and easily-molded schist, typical for Ephesos, is clearly visible on the south wall. Again, the floor and wall are covered by marble slabs, while the upper zone is filled in with painting. An erotes garland frieze extends across a white background above a socle zone, where theater masks inserted inside rhombi and rectangles decorated with horizontal ornament bands alternate. The flying, naked erotes are carrying a heavy and richly filled fruit garland that is crossed by a fine yellow garland hanging from decorated peltae. An ornamental band with a perspectival design separates the central zone from architectural painting located above in the vault, but only a few fragments are still preserved. Two openings remained unbarred to provide the room with light. The lunette continues the motif of the architectural painting. In the center, Victoria is standing in an aedicula with a pitched roof and surrounded on either side by additional aediculae. The carefulness of the production and the rich details of the images suggest that they were made by a workshop with great skill in the second quarter of the 3rd century in Terrace House 2. Their activities were not limited to residential unit 6, since identical wall systems are also located in other houses.

Remember this erotes garland frieze for the rest of the tour! Sadly, the fish basin that was once integrated into the north wall of the room and was decorated with its namesake décor is no longer visible. Supplied with fresh water through a canal, it was used for holding edible and decorative fish.

Viewing Location 4

You will now access the second story over an ancient staircase (32a), featuring a wall with stucco ashlar blocks of marble imitation in red frames. From here you will be able to take a look at the breathtaking panorama over residential unit 6. The addition of the bath (M1-3) in the east walkway of the peristyle courtyard (31a) in AD 120 can be easily understood. In this process, the columns were fully encapsulated and the newly constructed wall surface was covered with marble and wall paintings. The bathing rooms, connected with the courtyard through multiple glass windows, were closed after the destructions in AD 270/280. These walls were set against the debris that at this point already covered the courtyard by a couple meters. The bath at this time was no longer used for cleaning, but instead its furnishings were removed and it was used as a storage space.

Looking to the southeast over the marble hall (31), the courtyard with the groin vault (36) and the apsidal hall (8) give an impression of the former glamour of this formal area of residential unit 6. The second story was in no way inferior to the first story in regard to the quality of its furnishings. A room in the south (32) is decorated with marble floors and walls, and in the floor two small openings are visible that provided the lower vaulted room with light but also enabled communication. For example, it would have been possible to lower baskets filled with fruits into the lower room.

A glance to the south will reward you with a view into a formal room (25) of the next-higher terrace in residential unit 5. It is decorated with unusual wall decoration from the 3rd century AD. The elongated red fields are designed in plastic stucco with white frames and set above a green socle. The exclusive infrastructural furnishings of the upper story can also be seen in the poorly preserved room in the north east (36c1) that once had a floor heating system, as can be seen by the preserved hypocaust-pillars. The praefurnium (32c), the furnace, was located in the west. In the north of the upper story was a courtyard (32c/d) with preserved impressions in the mortar of the former marble tile floor. The lower-lying vault room (38c) was illuminated from here.

If you follow the corridor (37) to the west, you will see countless graffiti covering the wall painting of the south wall. The images etched into the wall represent gladiators, or more precisely heavily armed secutores. The high rectangular shield (scutum), the Roman short sword (gladius), the right arm protection (manica), and the leg guard (ocrea) can be clearly recognized. In addition to the depictions, etched inscriptions in Greek also cover the wall. On the left side of this space is a pithos sunk into the ground, where food was kept cool in order to keep it fresh longer. Behind it, in the southeast corner, is an area with multiple layers of wall paintings and mortar that accumulated over the centuries.

Viewing Location 5

From here you can look down into the large peristyle courtyard (38b) of residential unit 7. Its impluvium was covered with marble while the ambulatories in the west, north and east were decorated with mosaic floors. The decorative areas are designed like tri-colored carpets. The columns had Doric capitals and were connected with a wooden architrave. The entrance to the house was located in the west, but this area was heavily damaged by later building activities. The walls of the courtyard were furnished with wall paintings of which multiple phases have survived. While the older layers also featured figural décor, the uppermost and youngest layers consisted of imitation white marble slabs in green frames.

In the south is a large exedra (38) with a once-luxurious design. Marble slabs were mounted on the walls and floor. The upper zone of stucco décor was set off by a molded, plastic ledge. At one point niches structured the walls, but only one wide niche is preserved in the east wall while the others were closed up. If you look carefully, you can see multiple plaster layers of the earlier lining on the west wall.

A high, arched niche in the south wall –from the visitor walkway this is hard to see– was used for formal presentations of the busts of the emperor Tiberius and his mother Livia as well as a bronze sculpture of a snake. This ensemble corresponds with the altar and the table that are set up in the center of the courtyard. On the high round altar an eagle, the heraldic animal of the god Zeus/Jupiter but also of the Roman imperial house, is depicted in relief. The massive table, set on four legs with feet designed as lions' paws, has a board game etched into its table top. The conscious staging of altar, table, and portraits within this private house can probably be interpreted as signs of ritual veneration of the imperial family, in particular the Julio-Claudian dynasty.

Two wells, one in the north walkway of the courtyard, the other in the exedra in the south, provided access to ground water. The room east of the exedra (38a) has a very simple mosaic décor that consists of randomly-strewn, dark stones on a light background. The wall painting, a rough, lesene-system décor with architectural painting in the upper zone, suggests that this was a side room. In contrast, multiple rooms in the east have a more formal character. The only partially visible arched room (38c) is especially well preserved, with a central light opening, a painted coffer ceiling, and walls with marble revetment.

The windows and doors of the two rooms adjoining in the north opened onto the peristyle courtyard, where the architectural painting on a white background is put on display. In the front room (32e), erotes appear as emblems, in the back room (38d) are depictions of offering scenes as well as busts of the god Dionysus. The consequences of the large earthquake around AD 270/280 are particularly impressive here: shifts and waves in the mosaic of the walkway are results of the catastrophe as are the wall paintings darkened by soot in the eastern rooms. To the north of the courtyard (38b) was a multi-room bath suite (38e and h) that included a large basin; its back side was built into the northern walkway. Numerous northern rooms of the residential unit are very poorly preserved and have partially eroded.

The upper story was accessed over a staircase (39) in the southwest corner of the peristyle courtyard (38b), while a second entrance from stepped alley 3 possibly led directly up into the upper story; the entrance was approximately there where the door still is today. The utility rooms (33, 34a-b) were located in the upper story, including a latrine (34), as were other formal areas. In addition to the central courtyard, which had an upper row of columns, another courtyard (32c/d) supported by columns was found in the east. Between the first and second floor, the owner of residential unit 7 had a living space of over 1000 m^2.

The second story continued to be used after the earthquake destruction. The reuse of spolia, or older building elements, was typical for the later building phases. The structure of the building was not completely compromised until the construction of the early Byzantine craftsman quarter. This impressive and well-preserved quarter dominated the entire west side. A mill room (35) was built into the upper story of residential unit 7 and was entered from the south. A sophisticated system of water canals with strong calcium deposits led to the north towards further grain mills as well as a stone mill workshop (WT 1-2) located behind the tall, large, curved wall.

Viewing Location 6

A view back across residential unit 7 is rewarding. The platform also gives you an opportunity to look at the modern roofing structure more closely. It is a steel construction that rests on central pillars so that it is only minimally invasive. A highly durable, textile roof membrane is stretched across the steel frame and the vents along the sides aid the constant air circulation and well-balanced room climate. The construction of the protective structure not only secured the ancient houses and make the 4,000 m^2 ruins accessible to visitors, but has also made it possible preservation work and research all year round.

Viewing Location 7

While going up the stairs to the next platform, take a look to your right, where heavy calcium deposits can be seen in the early Byzantine water canals. You are now standing on the middle terrace, where residential units 3 and 5 are located. The platform itself is set inside the former industrial courtyard (27). From here, a corridor of residential unit 5 decorated with wall paintings was once entered. In the east of the courtyard is a small praefurnium that was used for heating the next room. An open fire in the living area was always a large danger and so it is understandable that this furnace chamber was separated from the courtyard by a wall; additionally, water was available close by. The heated formal room (26) had a hypocaust floor heating system with brick pillars and was decorated with marble floors and walls. A fountain still exists in the well-preserved south wall, but the basin once located in front of it is no longer there. The supply pipe of the fountain, as well as the drainage through a hole in the south-east corner of the marble floor, is still easily visible. The formal room (25) with stucco behind this has already been discussed.

Both rooms opened onto the peristyle courtyard (24) of residential unit 5. Multiple phases of the wall decoration are still preserved on the east wall: the older paintings show two medallions with portraits of philosophers on a white background. The individuals represented are named by inscriptions as Socrates (the Athenian) and Chilon (the Lacedaemonian/Spartan). Above that is a painting with red background that is partially covered by a marble revetment of the 3rd century AD. In order to help the next decorative surface adhere better, the older layer was roughened up, as can be seen by the dents from pickaxes on the surface of the wall.

A room (18) could be entered from the corridor as well as the courtyard and is today referred to as the 'erotes room'. A low socle decorated with red panels with lozenges and yellow panels with horizontal leaf garlands is located below a large main zone of lesene-system paintings. In the multi-frame panels, flying erotes can be seen on a white background holding garlands, wreaths, musical instruments, torches, and dishes for special events, offering these to guests entering from the peristyle courtyard. The décor above, set off by a perspectival decorative band, is very poorly preserved.

The east wall of the room deserves special attention. A wooden staircase was located here that led up into the second floor as can be seen by the plaster. The walls of the staircase were decorated with simple paintings that imitate ashlar masonry.

Looking straight ahead to the south, you will see the peristyle courtyard of residential unit 3 (16b) with fountains in the central niches and the rooms beyond decorated with wall painting (16a). The first room is the so-called lion room (17) that was entered through the peristyle courtyard (16b). An adjoining niche in the east is covered with paintings of scattered flowers. The namesake floor decoration of room 17 depicts a part of an amphitheater scene: the victorious lion is holding the head of the slain bull in his paws. The figural image is surrounded by a guilloche and a wide ornamental strip in the east emphasizes the unique orientation of the mosaic field of the east wall, in front of which a kline was probably set up. The walls have simple lesene-system paintings above a low socle and various birds are set into emblems.

Viewing Location 8

You have arrived at one of the most impressive locations in Terrace House 2, with a panoramic view across the central terrace with residential units 3 and 5 in the front and residential unit 4 in the back. To the west you can again see the water canals with extensive calcium deposits and the attached mill room (B17) is located exactly underneath the visitor path. It was built into a Roman formal room and only the frame of a mosaic –probably once with a figural image– remains.

The main focus though is in the east. Originally, a large house with two courtyards stood here and probably in the course of the 2nd century AD it was divided. The courtyard in the front (16b) belongs to the very small but very individualized residential unit 3 that was surrounded by corridors on three sides and provided access to the adjoining rooms. In the south, a fountain is set into a niche that was built between two columns and supplied with water through lead pipes. The rooms grouped around the courtyard, revetted with marble, were impressive due to the careful interior decorating with figural mosaics and wall paintings. Across from the already discussed lion room (17), located in the north, was an elongated large room that was divided into two smaller square rooms with identical decoration (16a) from the last building phase (around AD

230). These construction activities can be especially well demonstrated with the help of the wall painting on the south wall. While the older layers –scattered flowers and lesene-system paintings– still continue on, the last painting layer –a marble imitation of white slabs in red frames– already respects the dividing wall. The architectural painting in the upper zone has been exceptionally well preserved on the south wall of the eastern room: a winged figure appears in the center, accompanied by garlands that are hanging from kantharoi. If you look at the east wall carefully, you will still see numerous etched inscriptions that are tallies, rows of alphabets and accounts. The flooring in both rooms was done with care, adorned with figural mosaics. The busts of the god Dionysus and Medusa in front of the aegis were featured as central emblems and glass and gold stones were used.

The probably best-known room in Terrace House 2 is the so-called room of the muses (12) of residential unit 3, not least due to its restored surfaces. Above a low socle with a red meander and inscribed green cruciform flowers were the main panels with the namesake images. Designed as the central emblems and with inscriptions naming them, the nine muses –Clio, Euterpe, Thalia, Melpomene, Terpsichore, Erato, Polyhymnia, Urania, and Calliope– are depicted with their typical attributes. The cycle finishes on the south wall where the god of the muses, Apollo, is depicted along with the lyric poet Sappho as the tenth muse. The well-preserved upper zone of the south wall is filled with architectural paintings. While a theater scene is set in the central aedicula, painted statues of naked youths, probably imagined to be of bronze, are set in side aediculae.

The north wall of the room deserves special consideration. Here you can clearly recognize that the last layer of paint, that of the muse cycle, was painted onto already heavily deformed walls. This phenomenon is the result of the earthquake that shook Ephesus in the first half of the 3rd century AD and made a refurnishing of the Terrace House necessary.

The clay tile floor of the room of the muses is unusual. Likewise the two marble bases do not appear to have had any load-bearing function but simply were decorative and possibly were used to set up ornamental vases.

After the division of the two residential units, residential unit 5, located in the east, could be reached through a long, narrow corridor (27). In the center of the house was a peristyle courtyard (24) with columns that had fine Corinthian capitals. In the south was an adjoining marble-revetted exedra (13); in the north were two large, formal rooms. In addition to the already mentioned room of the erotes (18) in the west, another room (12a) should be mentioned because its painted wall decoration imitates veined marble slabs. All the way in the back, you can see a floor mosaic on the apse of the large hall of residential unit 6 that was part of the second story of residential unit 4.

Viewing Location 9

After ascending another set of steps, you will reach the uppermost terrace and residential unit

2. The small courtyard (SR 27) is surrounded by four fluted columns with Doric capitals. A mill room (B 16) impinges on the ancient material and meter-high walls built of numerous spolia –fragments of Corinthian and Ionic capitals as well as fluted column drums are recognizable– were set against the debris. The ambulatories of the courtyards were covered with mosaic floors, the walls decorated with simple lesene-system paintings, but this time birds and fish appear as emblems. Traces of intense fire on the walls are the result of the destruction in the 3rd century AD and show that a great fire broke out following the earthquake. In the south walkway of the courtyard, a kitchen (SR 27a) was installed but it was entered from the large peristyle courtyard (SR 22/23). The walled stove and the water installations are part of the standard equipment of kitchens that are only seldom found in Terrace House 2. Across from the kitchen is a small latrine (SR 29) with an entrance spanned by an arch. In front of the walled bench you can see a channel on the floor that provided fresh water and could be used for personal hygiene and cleaning purposes. The latrine could be used by at least three people at once. The walls are covered with caricatures of philosophers as well as etched inscriptions that directly refer to the use of the latrine. Those seated here are reminded not to remain too long.

A last ascent takes you to the highest visitor platform. On the way you walk across a small cubiculum (SR 25) that opens onto the large peristyle courtyard (SR 22/23) in the east. Above the door a small window is mounted up high that was not only used for lighting but also for the air circulation of the room. The floor is covered by a mosaic with a central emblem made of fine mosaic tiles while the outer frame is roughly made. The wall painting with white background follows the common lesene-system with birds and flower garlands in the panels and architectural paintings in the upper zone. The holes of the beams for the wooden ceiling are clearly visible on the south wall. A threshold shows that the room located in the story above opened up onto the street – it could have been a taberna situated along the Terrace House Street.

While walking up the steps, don't forget to look through the stairs into the large peristyle courtyard (SR 22/23) of residential unit 2. Here you will see the magnificent Amphitrite mosaic on the floor, the walls with marble revetment, and a frieze of erotes and garlands on a blue background. As an observant visitor you might be able to recall the decoration in the vaulted room in residential unit 6 where this motif was already pointed out – albeit on a white background: the painters working in the Terrace House in the 3rd century AD left their traces on all three terraces. Sadly the luxurious design of the exedra (GEW D) adjoining in the south of the courtyard can barely be seen. The splendor of the figural glass mosaic placed in the vault and the lunette can only be imagined from this location.

Viewing Location 10

From the uppermost platform you can look across residential unit 2: directly underneath the visitor path is the southern walkway of the peristyle courtyard (SR 22/23) with the mosaic of Amphitrite and the erotes-garland frieze. Wooden beams of the ceiling were mounted in the row of beam holes in the south wall, while of the staircase leading up into the second story, five steps still remain in the south-west corner of the courtyard.

The center of the splendidly-furnished peristyle courtyard is a circle of monolithic columns with Corinthian capitals. The impluvium was separated from the surrounding ambulatories by medium-high parapet walls. In the open courtyard area, a channel on all four sides drained off the rain water into canals below ground. The entire architectural ensemble as well as the wall revetment of the courtyard was made of marble that brought out its decorative aspects; the floors of the walkway were decorated with polychrome mosaics in geometric motifs.

The small cubicula (SR 25 and 26) adjoining in the west were furnished more simply but do not forego floor mosaics and wall painting. Based on the wall décor these are the so-called bird rooms. From the courtyard, multiple rooms for formal use could be entered in the north and east. This included a room (SR 28) in the north that had a narrow door and a wide interior window. The walls feature painted imitation of marble slabs which is typical for the 3rd century AD and can be seen in a variety of instances in Terrace House 2; the floor is covered by a black-white mosaic. The second northern room (SR 24) can be clearly identified as a triclinium based on the characteristic mosaic floor. The decorative areas were left blank where the klinai once stood. A wide, collapsible door connected this room with the courtyard and two niche fountains set into the south wall provided the room with water, but they are not visible from the visitor pathway.

In the northeast is an elongated room (SR 19/20) with paintings of the favorite motif of Terrace House 2: muses. But these are very poorly preserved in comparison with those of residential unit 3 and were also badly charred. Two niches in the wall with painted scattered flowers have traces of mounted shelves where scrolls were piled. Another formal room (SR 17) in the east was also connected with the peristyle courtyard through a wide doorway. The stucco decoration here belongs to some of the finest in Terrace House 2. White stucco frames formed in the round define high, rectangular fields above a low, green socle zone. From this room another room (SR 12) lying beyond could be reached, but it was poorly lighted and very simply furnished. It and the adjoining room (SR 16) appear to have been utility and storage rooms.

Viewing Location 11

If you look back onto the peristyle courtyard (SR 22/23) of residential unit 2, from here you will look exactly at the southern arcade. The four columns with brick arches are quite different than the others in the courtyard. They were set together out of spolia, vary in height and have different capitals. This arcade was not part of Roman interior decoration, but instead was added in Late Antiquity. The rooms in the north still belonged to residential unit 2 with the usual wall décor, i.e. the scattered flowers (SR 14), a lesene-system with flowers (SR 15) or hunting erotes (SR 18) as central emblems. Room SR 18 was named the ivory room due to its exquisite interior furnishings. Its mosaic floor is also worth looking at in greater detail: the carpet-like square emblem panel is centrally located and consists of small black-and-white mosaic stones while the outer frame is made of far rougher stones. The west wall has an arched niche with strewn-flower décor. A figural panel of a reclining, lightly dressed nymph cannot be seen from the visitor pathway.

In the background you can view the massive apse of the hall (8) of residential unit 6, and also the 2nd floor mosaic lying above it from residential unit 4.

If you continue walking to the east you will see the north rooms of residential unit 1. It had three entrances in its last phase of use: the main entrance (SR 1) was located at about the middle of the house along the stepped alley 1. A staircase led down into a small, open entrance courtyard (SR 1). The two wells lying on top of each other are impressive. They are made of bricks but the slab at the front of the basin is made of marble. Adjoining in the north on the side is a small access to a latrine (SR 1a). The industrial rooms in the north east were accessed separately (SR 4) and were in charge of stoking the furnace for the large bath (SR 3). The bath has all of the important elements of an ancient bath: a praefurnium with a long heating channel, a suspensura above pilae, a flue system in the wall, a bathing basin in the northeast corner, a testudo to quickly heat up water, as well as a wash basin in the niche in the southwest. The marble imitation of the last building phase can be easily recognized on the east wall; earlier the bath was furnished with real marble. It is very likely that the room was covered with a vault and glass windows.

The peristyle (SR 2) was the heart of the house with its four slightly fluted columns and oddly undecorated capitals. The north walkway was sectioned off in building phase IV (around AD 230) and two, almost square cubicula (SR 10a and b) were installed here. Both rooms have similar furnishing: black-white mosaic floors, lesene-system paintings with hunting erotes as central emblems on the walls, and niches in the north wall for the display of sculpture. Only the platform built in the northeast corner of room SR 10a does not exist in the neighboring room. It was used for placing dishes but also for setting up a coal brazier in the cold seasons.

Viewing Location 12

The center of the peristyle courtyard (SR 2) of residential unit 1 was the impluvium, separated from the ambulatories with medium-high parapet walls. In the north, a large spillover fountain was added that was structured by two wall niches. In contrast to most other residential units, the walls of the courtyard are not revetted with marble but instead were painted with a red background. The mosaic floors follow the familiar system: on a white background, long rectangular decorative panels are set in three colors. The high quality and well preserved mosaic floor in the exedra (GEW C) adjoining in the south can only be seen directly under the visitor pathway.

As a conclusion to the tour through Terrace House 2, let us take a look into the so-called theater room (SR 6) located to the east of the courtyard (SR 2). Of the unique wall decoration, it is only possible to see the upper zone of the paintings, with the depiction of the Philoctetes myth as the central image; the life-size servant figures and the theater scenes remain hidden from the Terrace House visitors. From the theater room small cubicula (GEW A and B) in the south could be entered. In the southwest corner of the peristyle (SR 2), a narrow staircase led up into the second story where the modern exit from the Terrace House 2 is located.

A final, thorough look across this unique monument of Roman private architecture is rewarding. While touring 4,000 m² of houses over three terraces it is possible to discuss various aspects of ancient living. It is rare for a visitor of archaeological sites to get so close to the ancient inhabitants as here.

After leaving Terrace House 2, you will step onto the original cobblestones of the Terrace House Street. The visitor path first turns to the west and further over stepped alley 3 to the north; once there, walk down the stairs to the downtown area of Ephesos. Having walked through the gate of Hadrian, you are now standing on the square of the library and have an impressive view of the resurrected façade of the library of Celsus.

Visitor Information

The archaeological site of Ephesos, Terrace House 2 and the archaeological museum (Efes Müzesi) in Selçuk are opened all year. Terrace House 2 is located in the center of the archaeological site and can be reached from the upper entrance over the agora and the Curetes Street as well as from the lower entrance over the Arkadiane and the Marble Street by foot in about 10 minutes. In both cases the modern structure is visible from afar. The Terrace Houses require a separate entrance fee and the tickets can be purchased by the booth at the entrance to the Terrace House. The visitor path through Terrace House 2 incorporates a couple very steep steps and best suited for visitors who are sure afoot. Numerous finds, including the rich furnishings and sculptures are on exhibit in the archaeological museum in Selçuk.

Hours May-October
Ephesos: 8 am to 6.30 pm
Terrace House 2: 8 am to 5.30 pm
Efes Müzesi Selçuk: 8.30 am to 6.30 pm

Hours November-April
Ephesos: 8 am to 5 pm
Terrace House 2: 8 am to 4.30 pm
Efes Müzesi Selçuk: 8.30 to 5 pm

Further Reading

T. Bezeczky, The amphorae of Roman Ephesus, Forschungen in Ephesos 15, 1 (Wien 2013).

M. Dawid, Die Elfenbeinplastiken aus dem Hanghaus 2 in Ephesos. Die Räume SR 18 und SR 28, Forschungen in Ephesos 8, 5 (Wien 2003).

W. Jobst, Römische Mosaiken in Ephesos I. Die Hanghäuser des Embolos, Forschungen in Ephesos 8, 2 (Wien 1977).

F. Krinzinger (ed.), Ein Dach für Ephesos. Der Schutzbau für das Hanghaus 2, Sonderschriften des Österreichischen Archäologischen Instituts 34 (Wien 2000).

F. Krinzinger (ed.), Das Hanghaus 2 von Ephesos: Studien zu Baugeschichte und Chronologie, Archäologische Forschungen 7 (Wien 2002).

F. Krinzinger (ed.), Hanghaus 2 in Ephesos. Die Wohneinheiten 1 und 2. Baubefund, Ausstattung, Funde, Forschungen in Ephesos 8, 8 (Wien 2010).

S. Ladstätter, Das Hanghaus 2 in Ephesos. Ein archäologischer Führer (Istanbul 2012) = S. Ladstätter, Yamaç Ev 2. Arkeolojik bir rehber (Istanbul 2012).

F. Mangartz, Die byzantinische Steinsäge von Ephesos. Baubefund, Rekonstruktion, Architekturteile, Monographien des Römisch-Germanischen Zentralmuseums 86 (Mainz 2010).

V. M. Strocka, Die Wandmalerei der Hanghäuser in Ephesos, Forschungen in Ephesos 8, 1 (Wien 1977).

H. Thür, Hanghaus 2 in Ephesos. Die Wohneinheit 4. Baubefund, Ausstattung, Funde, Forschungen in Ephesos 8, 5 (Wien 2005).

H. Thür – E. Rathmayr (ed.), Hanghaus 2 in Ephesos. Die Wohneinheit 6. Baubefund, Ausstattung, Funde, Forschungen in Ephesos 8, 9 (in print).

N. Zimmermann – S. Ladstätter, Wandmalerei in Ephesos von hellenistischer bis in byzantinische Zeit (Wien 2010) = N. Zimmermann – S. Ladstätter, Wall Painting in Ephesos from the Hellenistic to the Byzantine period (Istanbul 2011) = N. Zimmermann – S. Ladstätter, Efes duvar resimleri hellenistik dönemden bizans dönemine kadar (Istanbul 2011).

Up-to-date information can also be found on the following websites:

Austrian Archaeological Institute
<http://www.oeai.at>

Institute for the Study of Ancient Culture at the Austrian Academy of Sciences
<http://www.oeaw.ac.at/antike>

Society of the Friends of Ephesos
<http://www.ephesos.at>

Ephesus-Foundation
<http://www.ephesus-foundation.org>

Short Biography of the Excavator Hermann Vetters

Hermann Vetters (1915–1993) was part of the research team of the Ephesos excavations since 1960 and under the leadership of Fritz Eichler he played an important role in the excavation of the Terrace Houses 1 and 2. In 1969 he received an appointment at the University of Vienna where he held the professorship for Classical Archaeology with an emphasis on field archaeology and classics until his retirement in 1985. At the same time he became director of the Austrian Archaeological Institute and field director in Ephesos. Here he devoted himself to the excavation of Terrace House 2 which was successfully completed in 1985. From 1982–1991 Hermann Vetters was also the Vice-president of the Austrian Academy of Sciences. He is the author of numerous scientific publications on topics of Roman provincial archaeology and Ephesos. He is also credited with the anastylosis, the reconstruction, of the Celsus Library and the Mazeus and Mithridates Gate.

The Research Team of Terrace House 2

Numerous scholars and scientists are dedicated to the research of Terrace House 2. We are indebted to them for their work:

Adenstedt Ingrid (architecture)
Auinger Johanna (sculpture)
Aurenhammer Maria (sculpture)
Bezeczky Tamás (amphora)
Christof Eva (sculpture)
Dawid Maria (ivory)
Flessa Nicolas (egyptology)
Forstenpointner Gerhard (zooarchaeology)
Galik Alfred (zooarchaeology)
González Horacio (amphora)
Herold Karl (conservation)
İlhan Sinan (conservation marble hall)
Iro Daniel (excavation)
Jenewein Gunhild (architectural decoration)
Jilek Sonja (small finds)
Jobst Werner (mosaics)
Karwiese Stefan (excavation)
Koller Karin (marble)
Kowalleck Ireen (small finds)
Krinzinger Friedrich (protective structure)
Ladstätter Sabine (excavation, pottery)
Lang-Auinger Claudia (terracottas)
Mangartz Fritz (Byzantine workshops)
Michalczuk Johanna (wells)
Outschar Ulrike (excavation)
Pfisterer Matthias (coins)
Plattner Georg (architectural decoration)
Ployer René (excavation)
Popovtschak Michaela (archaeobotany)
Prochaska Walter (geology)

Quatember Ursula (stone objects)

Rathmayr Elisabeth (building analysis, small finds, sculpture)

Rudolf Ernst (excavation)

Sauer Roman (petrography)

Schätzschock Martina (glass)

Scheibelreiter-Gail Veronika (mosaics)

Schindel Nikolaus (coins)

Schwaiger Helmut (excavation)

Sokolicek Alexander (excavation)

Steskal Martin (excavation)

Strocka Volker-Michael (paintings)

Taeuber Hans (epigraphy)

Thanheiser Ursula (archaeobotany)

Thür Hilke (building analysis)

Tober Barbara (paintings)

Trinkl Elisabeth (small finds)

Waldner Alice (pottery)

Weber Johannes (archaeometry)

Weissengruber Gerald (zooarchaeology)

Wefers Stefanie (Byzantine workshops)

Wiplinger Gilbert (water technology)

Zimmermann Norbert (paintings)

Acknowledgements

It is a great joy to finally be able to present Terrace House 2, an impressive monument of Roman private life, to an interested audience after years of intense study. The realization of the project was only possible through the cooperation of many people. I would like to explicitly thank the scientific team at the Austrian Academy of Sciences in Vienna that has been extensively engaged with the topic for decades and where I was a member for many years. I am grateful to Andreas Pülz, the director of the Institute for the Study of Ancient Culture at the Austrian Academy of Sciences, for his support and his permission to publish numerous plans and reconstruction drawings. The Austrian Archaeological Institute in Vienna has provided excellent working conditions for the production of the manuscript and only through the access to numerous archival records, in particular the large image database, was it possible to achieve a higher standard. I am also indebted to the Turkish authorities that trust us every year and thus make it possible for us to do our work. Especially Cengiz Topal, the director of the Efes Müzesi in Selçuk, must be thanked for the smooth and unbureaucratic progress of the excavation seasons.

Numerous colleagues greatly supported this project by providing information, images or preparing pictures and plans: I would like to thank Falko Daim, Nicolas Gail, Marc Grellert, Sinan İlhan, Christian Kurtze, Filiz Öztürk, Gottfried Parrer, Mieke Pfarr, Walter Prochaska, Elisabeth Rathmayr, Martin Steskal, Hans Taeuber, Özlem Vapur, Alice Waldner, Stefanie Wefers und Norbert Zimmermann. Above all, I am deeply grateful to Barbara Beck-Brandt for her careful editing: without her this book project would not have been possible.

This English version of the guide published in German and Turkish in 2012 is now being released with the publisher Homer Kitabevi. I would like to thank Ms. Ayse Boylu for including this book in its publication series and for the attentive handling of the publishing process. Special thanks are due to the translators Nicole

M. High and Emma Sachs. The financial support of the Ephesus-Foundation made the publication possible. I am especially grateful to the president of the foundation, Ahmet Kocabiyik, and its manager, Gülsevim Avci Tolunay.

The financial support of the Federal Ministry for Science and Research as well as the Austrian Science Fund has made the research and work in Ephesos, especially Terrace House 2, possible. In addition, the patronage of our sponsor is significant: the Society of the Friends of Ephesos, based in Vienna, facilitated the construction of the protective structure over Terrace House 2 in addition to many other projects; the Borusan-Holding based in Istanbul financed the restoration of the marble hall (31) of residential unit 6; the conservation of the wall paintings in Terrace House 2 has been made possible by the Ephesus-Foundation, also based in Istanbul. Helmut Schwaiger not only frequently encouraged me to write a guide book to Terrace House 2 but also helped me considerably while writing it. I dedicate this book to him and our daughter Hemma.

Glossary

Aedicula	small architectural framework, similar to a temple front
Aegis	shield of the goddess Athena
Acclamation	calling out, expression of approval
Apodyterium	dressing room
Apsidiole	a small apse, semi-round niche with corner arc
Aqueduct	water channel
Architrave	beam resting on columns, part of the entablature
Asiarch	high Roman official in the province Asia
Barrel vault	vault with semi-circular shape
Basilica	originally audience hall of king then large building for jurisdiction and commerce
Breccia	type of stone
Buskin	high, thick-soled boot of actors
Caldarium	warm bath
Caryatid	female architectural support
Cella	here: private room, otherwise: inside of a temple with the cult image
Centaur	creature of Greek mythology, half horse, half human
Chora	agriculturally used countryside
Cipollino verde	green marble from the island Euboea
Clients	supporters; individuals faithful, reliant and committed to a patron
Convivium	meal in the evening
Cubiculum	side room, usually for sleeping
Damnatio memoriae	condemnation of memory
Dipinto	painted inscription

Double aulos	musical instrument, similar to the double flute, played with both hands
Emblem	single picture, can be inserted
Epigram	label, concise poem
Exedra	niche-like room
Fluting	vertical grooves along the column shaft
Graffito	etched inscription
Greco scritto	type of marble from the vicinity of Ephesos
Frigidarium	Cold bathing room
Hippocamp	mythological creature of sea, part horse, part fish
Hypocaust	floor heating system
Impluvium	flat water basin designed to catch and drain water, in the center of the peristyle courtyard or atrium
In situ	left in the original location
Insula	here: house block, parcel surrounded on all sides by streets
Kantharos	drinking vessel with two handles
Kline	Roman reclining couch
Labrum	wash basin
Latrine	toilet
Lesene	upright rectangular ornament field
Lunette	upper part of wall with semi-circular shape and surrounded by vault

Marble incrustation	wall/facade revetment with marble slabs
Monolitic	made out of one piece (marble, stone)
Neocorate	honorary right to construct a temple for the Imperial cult
Nereids	daughters of Nereus, nature spirit
Nymphaeum	sanctuary above springs or wells, noble buildings at the mouth of a water chanal
Oculus, oculi	central opening for light
Oolith	sedimentary rock
Opus mixtum	wall of ruble and brick layers
Opus sectile	floors of cut marble pieces
Opus signinum	waterproof floor surface
Oscilla	hanging decorative elements, often in the shape of masks
Patron	house owner
Pavonazetto	a white marble with dark veins and inclusions
Peltae	crescent-shape, originally form of a shield
Peristyle	courtyard with columns
Peristyle house	house with a columnar courtyard
Pilae	small stacks of tiles for floor heating
Pithos	large storage container
Plinth	socle
Porfido rosse	purple porphyry
Porfido verde	green porphyry
Praefurnium	furnace chamber
Prytanis	high official of the city government
Puteal	type of water well wellhead
Salutatio	morning greeting
Spolia	older construction elements, reused in newer buildings

SR	south room
Stoa	here: covered portico
Sudatorium	sweat bath
Suspensura	heated floor resting on pillars (pilae)
Symposium	party, ritualized drinking event
Taberna	shop, tavern
Tegula mammata	rectangular tile with conical projections or flanges at each corner on one side
Tepidarium	warm bath
Tessera,-ae	mosaic stone
Testudo	furnace
Thiasos of the sea	procession of the retinue of the god of the sea
Thymiaterium	incense altar
Togatus	statue or depiction of a man wearing the Roman costume
Triclinium	dining room
Triton	Greek sea god, son of Poseidon and Amphitrite
Tubulus	hollow brick, used as a heat conductor

Sources of Illustrations

Fig. 1–15. 17–20. 22–23. 25–30. 32–42. 46–47. 49–50. 52. 54–57. 60–65. 68–83. 85–87. 89. 90. 92–94. 96–101. 103–113. 115–122. 124. 126–154. 156–158. 160–221. 223. 225–236: © Österreichisches Archäologisches Institut

Fig. 12: © Kunsthistorisches Museum Wien

Fig. 16. 44. 88. 95. 102. 114. 123. 159. 222. 224: © Österreichische Akademie der Wissenschaften, Institut für Kulturgeschichte der Antike

Fig. 21. 53. 58: © Technische Universität Darmstadt

Fig. 24: © Technische Universität Wien

Fig. 31: © E. Wunderer, Wien

Fig. 43. 45. 48. 51. 66–67. 84. 91. 125. 155. 239: © Österreichisches Archäologisches Institut / Österreichische Akademie der Wissenschaften, Institut für Kulturgeschichte der Antike

Fig. 59. 237. 238: © Römisch-Germanisches Zentralmuseum Mainz

Fig. 156: © Veterinärmedizinische Universität Wien